GHOST STORIES
of Illinois

Jo-Anne Christensen

LONE PINE

© 2000 by Jo-Anne Christensen and Lone Pine Publishing
First printed in 2000   10 9 8 7 6 5 4 3 2
Printed in Canada

All rights reserved. No part of this work covered by the copyrights hereon may be reproduced or used in any form or by any means—graphic, electronic or mechanical—without the prior written permission of the publisher, except for reviewers, who may quote brief passages. Any request for photocopying, recording, taping or storage on information retrieval systems of any part of this work shall be directed in writing to the publisher.

The Publisher: Lone Pine Publishing

10145 - 81 Avenue	1901 Raymond Ave. SW, Suite C
Edmonton, AB T6E 1W9	Renton, WA 98055
Canada	USA

Website: www.lonepinepublishing.com

Canadian Cataloguing in Publication Data
Christensen, Jo-Anne.
   Ghost stories of Illinois

Includes bibliographical references.
ISBN 1-55105-239-3

   1. Ghosts—Illinois. 2. Legends—Illinois. I. Title.
GR580.C57 2000   398.25'09773   C00-910531-X

Editorial Director: Nancy Foulds
Project Editor: Eli MacLaren
Production Manager: Jody Reekie
Book Design: Monica Triska
Layout & Production: Arlana Anderson-Hale

Photos Courtesy of: Chicago Public Library Special Collections and Preservation Division (p. 15, p. 22); University of Illinois at Chicago, University Library, Special Collections (JAMC neg. 163, p. 33); Dennis Shappka (p. 60, p. 62, p. 85, p. 113, p. 117, p. 159, p. 188); Eastland Disaster Historical Society (p. 68); Donald L. Barnett (p. 74, p. 93, p. 95); Quincy University, Brenner Library (p. 76, p. 164); Steve Anderson, Fort de Chartres State Historic Site (p. 107, p. 108); Galena Historical Society and Museum (p. 219, p. 223).

We acknowledge the financial support of the Government of Canada through the Book Publishing Industry Development Program (BPIDP) for our publishing activities.

PC: P6

Dedication

For my sweet Gracie Bundle.

Contents

Acknowledgments

No one writes a book alone. I would like to thank the many kind and generous individuals who have helped me along the way.

My first thanks go to the creative and dedicated staff at Lone Pine Publishing. I have been so very pleased by your professionalism and support. In particular, my editor, Eli MacLaren, deserves credit for using his sharp eye and considerable skill to make this book so much better than it would otherwise have been.

W. Ritchie Benedict of Calgary is an endlessly generous and brilliant researcher—sometimes producing nearly impossibly obscure material as if by magic. Thank you so much, Ritchie! The equally talented Dr. Barrie Robinson of Edmonton was kind enough to read through reams of rough material, in order to provide me with some fresh insight into two time-worn stories.

The majority of the research was made so much easier by those guardians of our past, the many helpful individuals employed at the museums, libraries and historical societies of Illinois. Specific thanks are owed to Patricia Tomczak of Quincy University's Brenner Library, Andrea Telli of the Chicago Public Library's Special Collections and Preservation Division, Donald L. Barnett of the Fulton County Historical and Genealogical Society, Don Parker of the Hancock County Historical Society, and Ted Wachholz of the Eastland Disaster Historical Society. The last organization can be contacted at the following address:

Eastland Disaster Historical Society
P.O. Box 2013
Arlington Heights, IL 60006-2013
http://www.eastlanddisaster.org
info@eastlanddisaster.org

I must also give credit to those who have gone before me in this field. Many talented paranormal investigators and folklorists, often local experts, significantly enriched my experience as an author. I salute you and thank you.

Finally, I wish to express my heartfelt gratitude to those nearest and dearest to me. Their support is so unwavering that I'm ashamed to admit I often take it for granted. To my fellow author and very dear friend Barbara Smith, thank you for always believing and proving that two heads are better than one. I believe ours is the definitive "mutually beneficial" relationship. To my children, Steven and Grace, thank you for forgiving me all the long hours and missed play times. My ultimate gratitude, however, is reserved for my husband, Dennis. Your support and input have always been invaluable. Thank you for the ideas, thank you for the encouragement, and thank you for being my partner in every way. Without you, I would not be doing what I love.

Introduction

"It was a dark and stormy night."

There are reasons why this introductory line is a favorite among tellers of ghost stories. Within the space of a few words it conjures up drama, dread and mystery. We all love to be frightened—it satisfies some deep-seated need—and one of the things that frightens us is the unknown. Ghost stories are rife with mystery, but inexplicable phenomena are not their only attraction. When we read these stories, we are also reassured by the possibility that our spirits are eternal. From a literary perspective, ghost stories really are terrifically efficient. They manage to push all of our buttons at once.

The ghost story is an age-old genre that has recently been rejuvenated by an increasing interest in the question of whether or not ghosts actually exist. More and more people seem determined to study ghosts in a scientific fashion. Investigative organizations are springing up around the country and around the world, and a body of knowledge is slowly but surely accumulating.

Given the masses of folklore and growing scientific knowledge, can it be said that anyone truly understands ghosts? The answer would still seem to be "no": ghosts vary so widely in nature, appearance and effect, that no one definition can comprehend them all. Nevertheless, patterns of supernatural phenomena have led paranormal researchers to postulate different categories of hauntings. There are spirits who are apparently intelligent and aware. They react to the circumstances and people around them. There are other ghosts classed as "residual hauntings." They are less agents than imprints which someone has left upon his or her surroundings. For example, an old woman was accustomed to waking every night at 11 PM and walking down the stairs to the kitchen, where she would have tea and toast. For years after her death, the woman's family would hear her footsteps on the stairs, every night at exactly 11.

In many instances, specters continue about the business of their lives simply because they have not yet realized that they are dead. This often happens when death is sudden and unexpected. These phantoms become frustrated when they can't negotiate the physical landscape with their accustomed ease, and are understandably upset when other people move into their homes, jobs and even marriages.

Whatever kind of ghost you're looking for, you will find a wealth of convincing examples in Illinois. The Prairie State seems to be particularly haunted. Why that is, no one can say. Some paranormal investigators say that the Mississippi River and Lake Michigan are to blame, crediting the theory that running water nurtures psychic activity. Others point to the state's dramatic and often violent history. Some can't explain exactly why Illinois is so filled with paranormal activity, but simply accept that it is. On one occasion, famed psychic Joseph DeLouise spoke to author Brad Steiger about the power of the city of Chicago, in particular:

Certain areas seem to drain a person's psychic energies. Chicago replenishes them. And I'm seeing more and more people becoming affected in this way. The Chicago area has the vibrations conducive to psychic development, psychic research, and psychic phenomena—the entire spectrum of psi [psychic] activity.

When asked why, DeLouise went on to say that it's "something to do with clouds, the altitude of the city and the water in the lake."

Because Illinois is so very haunted, it would be virtually impossible to produce a truly comprehensive collection of its ghost stories. Instead, this book is what I believe to be a representative sampling of tales, including the famous, the never-before-told, the contemporary and the historical. (Some, I admit, made the cut simply because they are personal favorites.)

The question remains: are the stories true?

I believe that many are, and that most can be categorized as being true on some level. I'm a storyteller, however, not a paranormal investigator, and so will leave you to make those distinctions for yourself. I must add that the tales based on folklore rather than fact should not be dismissed. Their expression of the fears, superstitions and mores of a given time is just as valuable as the narration of a convincing supernatural event.

My sincere wish is that the following selections fulfill the traditional value of the ghost story. In other words, I hope that this book entertains you. Keep it close by, so that you can crack it open whenever you wish to be carried away to a mysterious place on a dark and stormy night.

These are the ghost stories of Illinois. Enjoy!

Chapter 1

HISTORICALLY
HAUNTED

*Some of the most fascinating and believable
ghost stories are those with historical roots.
The intriguing blend of indisputable facts and
elusive mysteries appeals to a wide audience.
Those who ordinarily might not partake of
paranormal fare find that archival records lend
a satisfying layer of texture and substance to the
ghost story. Similarly, people who find the usual
historical texts just a little on the dry side are
often drawn to the very same information, when
a tantalizing tale of terror is woven in.*

*In Illinois, there is plenty of material to please
both the history buffs and the paranormal
enthusiasts. The influx of the French, the havoc
of the Civil War, the Great Chicago Fire of 1871,
the gunfire of the gangster era—every period of
history has left its own distinct mark—
whether physical or psychic—on the Prairie State.*

*The following are a few of the ghosts that make
Illinois so very historically haunted.*

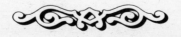

Abraham Lincoln and the Spirit World

On the morning of April 14, 1865, President Abraham Lincoln called a Cabinet meeting. He sat at the table in the council chamber as the members filed in, but for some time seemed not to notice them. Lincoln's face was buried in his hands. When he finally found the strength to raise his head, the expression on his face was one of utter anguish.

"Gentlemen," the President said, "before long you will have important news." When the men pressed Lincoln for details, he told them of a recurring dream that he'd had for the third time the night before. "It is always the same," he explained. "I am in a boat, alone on a boundless ocean. I have no oars, no rudder. I am helpless. I drift. Something extraordinary is going to happen, and very soon."

They were prophetic words, for that evening, during a performance of *Our American Cousin* at Ford's Theater, Lincoln was assassinated by a Southern sympathizer named John Wilkes Booth.

Abraham Lincoln is remembered as one of the greatest and most beloved leaders in American history. Among those who are interested in supernatural phenomena, he also stands apart as one of the most psychic. While numerous White House families have been known occasionally to rely on "alternative" guidance—think of the Reagans' use of astrologers, or Hillary Rodham Clinton's famous chats with Eleanor Roosevelt—Lincoln's faith in second sight and connection to the spirit world were no passing fancy. The President's beliefs were deeply ingrained; his clairvoyance was an integral part of his way of life. Throughout his life he consulted psychics and attended seances.

Abraham Lincoln, March 1861.

He paid close attention to premonitions and visions, and looked for meaning in his dreams. He took advice from those on the other side and felt guided, and even manipulated, by what he frequently referred to as "the hand of God." Moreover, as early as five years prior to his death, he knew that he would never serve out his second term as President of the United States.

Hours after his election in 1860, while Lincoln was waiting in Springfield, Illinois for the last report on the vote, he had a strange experience. He had retired to his quarters for a much-needed rest, and was reclining on a settee when he was startled by his reflection in a large mirror, opposite him. Lincoln later described the baffling sight to a friend: "My face, I noticed, had two separate and distinct images. One of the faces was a little paler—about five shades—than the other."

Lincoln stood up, and the image melted away. He lay down, and it returned. Every time he attempted to recreate the effect, (even days later) he was successful. Nevertheless, he was the only one who could see it. The President's wife, Mary Todd Lincoln, was disturbed by his account of the phenomenon. She believed that the corpse-like shadow her husband was projecting was an omen. According to her interpretation, the healthy, normal reflection represented Lincoln's first term in office. The paler, less substantial image symbolized a second term, which he would begin, but never finish.

10 days before his fateful outing to the theater, Lincoln had a dream that required much less interpretation. In his journal, he described it:

I retired late. I soon began to dream. There seemed to be a deathlike stillness about me. Then I heard subdued sobs, as if a number of people were weeping. I thought I left my bed and wandered downstairs. There the silence was broken by the same pitiful sobbing, but the mourners were invisible. I went from room to room; no living person was in sight, but the same mournful sounds of distress met me as I passed along.

It was light in all the rooms; every object was familiar to me; but where were all the people who were grieving as if their hearts would break? I was puzzled and alarmed. What could be the meaning of all this? Determined to find the cause of a state of things so mysterious and so shocking, I kept on until I arrived at the East Room, which I entered. Before me was a catafalque, on which rested a corpse wrapped in funeral vestments. Around it were stationed soldiers who were acting as guards; and there was a throng of people, some gazing mournfully upon the corpse, whose face was covered, others weeping pitifully. "Who is dead in the White House?" I demanded of one of the soldiers. "The President," was his answer. "He was killed by an assassin."

Given the psychic warning—not to mention the fact that Lincoln had received a number of death threats—one has to wonder why the President still insisted upon his lightly guarded outing to the theater on April 14, 1865. Perhaps Lincoln refused to lead a life ruled by the fear that must have resulted from such premonitions. Perhaps his fatalistic view of the universe led him to believe that no matter what choices he made, he could not alter what was meant to be. He once wrote in a letter to a friend that he often felt controlled "by some other power than [his] own will." And so it was. President Abraham Lincoln was warned, but not saved, by his psychic talents. He received a single gunshot to the back of his head, and expired within hours. The assassination would not be the end, however, for according to many reports, the late Lincoln was able to appear to the living as easily as the living man had communicated with the dead.

Lincoln's body was transported home to Springfield by train. Upon arrival, it was placed in a special receiving vault, near the beautiful mausoleum that was being constructed. Within days, the first reported sightings of the late President's ghost surfaced. He had been seen pacing the path between the temporary crypt and the mausoleum—a tall, thin, somber figure. If Lincoln's spirit was overseeing the project, its completion brought him no peace: after his remains were moved into their final resting place, visitors to the tomb were often disturbed by the sounds of sobbing and footsteps coming from within.

Abraham Lincoln's spirit seemed to be as tireless as was the man himself, and it soon became clear that he would not be limiting his ghostly visitations to Oak Ridge Cemetery. In death, Lincoln seemed anxious to haunt all the places that had been meaningful to him in life; his ghost became known as one of the most well-traveled citizens of the afterlife. His familiar, lanky frame and awkward gait have been identified many times in the dark, shadowy shape that walks the streets surrounding the old courthouse in Springfield. It was there that Lincoln pleaded numerous cases as a young lawyer. It has also long been rumored that the historical Lincoln Home in Springfield is haunted by him. There, a tall, thin apparition is accompanied by the ghost of a young boy. The man is no doubt Lincoln; the boy, very likely his beloved son Willie, who predeceased the President by three years.

Over the years, many well-documented sightings of Lincoln's ghost have been outside of Illinois, in the place where he spent the most dramatic years of his life.

The list of those who have seen or sensed Lincoln's presence in the White House is distinguished and long. Numerous presidents, including Roosevelt, Truman and Eisenhower, felt that the Great Emancipator still occupied many of the historic rooms where they worked and lived. Calvin Coolidge's wife, Grace, saw Lincoln's distinctive silhouette standing at a window in the Oval Office, gazing out over the Potomac. Since then, many others—including the famous poet Carl Sandburg—have reported seeing or feeling Lincoln's spirit in that same location.

Eleanor Roosevelt used Lincoln's former bedroom as a study. Often, as she was writing late at night, she would have the overwhelming sense that she was not alone. Looking over her shoulder, she would find no one there. Eventually she simply assumed that Lincoln was keeping her company.

Visitors to the White House have also been known to encounter the ghost of the 16th president. Winston Churchill—who was known to be influenced by premonitory visions of his own—is said to have seen Lincoln's ghost while on an official visit. During a visit to President Roosevelt, Queen Wilhelmina of the Netherlands was once awakened by a knocking at her bedroom door. She rose from her bed to open the door, and a moment later fell to the floor in a dead faint. There, waiting to be admitted, was the semitransparent figure of Abraham Lincoln.

Lincoln's persistent spiritual presence in the White House has often been explained as a residual effect of the enormous energy he expended there during the traumatic years of the Civil War. That concentration of emotion was matched by the sorrow the nation felt when he died. The funeral train that bore his body from Washington to Springfield was met, along its route, by more than seven million grieving Americans. This outpouring of sorrow must have left its own psychic mark, for a phantom version of that train is said to retrace its passage every year, on the anniversary of the somber journey.

The legend tells of two spectral steamers. The first pulls several cars that are draped in black. In one car, shadowy instruments play mournful dirges, while a macabre audience of skeletons looks on. The second engine pulls only a single flatbed car, which is covered in black carpeting and bears the coffin containing Lincoln's body. *The Albany Evening Times* once described the eerie change in atmosphere that was said to accompany the strange event:

> The air on the tracks becomes very keen and cutting. On either side of the tracks it is warm and still. Every watchman, when he feels the air, slips off the track and sits down to watch.

If a real train were passing its noise would be hushed as if the phantom train rode over it. Clocks and watches always stop as the phantom train goes by and when looked at are five to eight minutes behind.

Strangely, the ghost train allegedly never reaches Springfield. In Illinois—the state that calls itself the "Land of Lincoln"— Abraham Lincoln is still a formidable presence. His name graces countless organizations, and his home and tomb are perennial tourist draws. Beyond these immortalizing honors, however, Lincoln seems to have truly remained among us in spirit. For more than 135 years, his ghost has defied the grave.

In Lincoln's second inaugural address, given shortly before his assassination, he implored, "let us strive on, to finish the work we are in." Within weeks, his natural life was cut short—yet one can't help but wonder if Abraham Lincoln is not still walking among us, striving to finish that work.

The Great Chicago Fire

On Sunday, October 8, 1871, just after nine o'clock in the evening, a fire broke out in the barn behind the O'Leary home on DeKoven Street, in Chicago. Whether the O'Learys' now infamous cow or something else was to blame will never be known. What is certain is that the fire spread and grew with incredible speed, resulting in unimaginable destruction. It became one of the worst calamities in the city's history.

For two days, the flames leaped furiously from one structure to another, driven north and east through Chicago by a strong, dry wind. In a city built of wood—a city which had only seen three inches of rain all summer, and none of that in the three weeks preceding the fire—there was nothing but fuel in the path of the blaze. Houses, businesses and factories were all consumed. The Chicago River was no barrier; the flames jumped it easily and, at one point, the oil-slicked waterway itself began to burn. The streets were clogged with crowds of people salvaging their possessions, searching for lost loved ones and even carrying their own dead. It was a holocaust.

On the morning of October 10, merciful rain began to fall. The fire finally died, and the City of Chicago began to count its losses. The business district, in the heart of the city, had been entirely destroyed. The dead numbered over 300; the homeless, 100,000. Property damage was estimated at over $200 million. But though the devastation was great, the determination to overcome it was greater. Soon to be as famous as the fire itself was the indestructible spirit Chicagoans showed as they began to rebuild their city.

Within only a few days, basic services were being offered through temporary locations. Shacks and simple stands sprang up in the rubble, and business crept forward once again. Realtor William D. Kerfoot was a fine example of the city's spirit. The day after the fire ended, Kerfoot erected a shanty and reopened his business, with a hand-made sign that announced his name, address, and the following report: "All gone but WIFE, CHILDREN and ENERGY." Individuals like Kerfoot galvanized the reconstruction process, and within a few short years recovery was complete.

The buildings had been replaced and the city looked undamaged, but it would take a long time to erase the emotional scars. Vivid memories of the nightmare remained, and over the years, stories emerged.

Erie Street, Chicago. The city was almost entirely destroyed during the Great Fire of 1871.

The only structure in downtown Chicago to survive the blaze was the massive limestone water tower. As the fire raged, the tower must have appeared to be a safe, stone haven among the innumerable wooden tinder boxes. There are tales that many people, exhausted from running, may have sought refuge there. Unfortunately, the choking clouds of smoke would still have found them.

Since the fire, there have been numerous reports of phantom faces peering out from the high windows of the tower. They are perhaps the ghosts of those who suffocated while seeking refuge. Sometimes, a lifeless body can be seen hanging from a noose. Legend states that this figure, seen through an upper window, is the specter of a man who chose to hang himself, rather than be torturously consumed by the smoke and heat.

There is one other building that sat squarely in the path of the Great Fire and prevailed: Holy Family Church, at the corner of

Roosevelt Road and May Street, did not burn. Unlike the survival of the water tower, which was built of fire-resistant stone, the endurance of Holy Family Church was deemed a mystery—or miracle. The flames seemed simply to cut a path around the beautiful building, leaving it unscathed. Parishioners thanked Our Lady of Perpetual Help for intervening, while atheists scratched their heads in wonder.

Today, Holy Family Church is said to be haunted. Two young brothers who drowned in 1874 have often materialized before members of the congregation. Once, they appeared with lighted candles to fetch someone who could perform last rites for their dying mother. After delivering the priest to the woman's bedside, they vanished without a whisper.

The most inscrutable account involving these ghosts relates to the Great Fire. Apparitions of the children were said to have appeared to several parishioners, warning them of the impending danger. The ghosts were credited with saving many lives—a fascinating feat, because the fire in 1871 occurred three full years before the boys' deaths.

It seems that the true cause of the fire was only the first of many mysteries from those days, which will simply never be explained.

Capone's Bloody Valentine

"Only Capone kills like that."

This terse and unforgettable comment came from George "Bugs" Moran, following the infamous St. Valentine's Day Massacre of 1929. Although Capone retaliated in the press by accusing Moran in return, everyone knew Bugs was right. Alphonse "Scarface" Capone had masterminded the gruesome hit. It gave him control of Chicago's underground, and resulted, ultimately, in a psychic stain of violence that would never be erased.

The hit took place, that cold February morning, at a north side warehouse on Clark Street that served as the bootlegging headquarters for Moran's gang. Several men had gathered inside the red brick building with the sign that read "S-M-C Cartage Garage" to await a shipment of hijacked whiskey. Five, including Frank Gusenberg and James Clark, were hard-core members of Moran's outfit; the sixth, Johnny May, was an expert safecracker who worked as the group's mechanic for $50 a week; and the seventh, Reinhardt Schwimmer, was an optometrist who had recently become friendly with Moran, and enjoyed the excitement of keeping such notorious company.

May, accompanied that morning by his dog, Highball, was busy repairing a broken-down truck. The other men gathered around a hot plate, drinking coffee and shivering, as they waited for the arrival of their leader. What they did not know was that Bugs Moran had been close to the warehouse only moments earlier, but had spotted a police car and thought it best to leave. It was a move that saved the mobster from becoming a statistic in the greatest blood bath in Chicago's gangland history.

The police car that pulled up in front of the warehouse that morning was a fake. The four men who got out of the cruiser, including two in Chicago Police Department uniforms, were impostors. Nevertheless, they looked real enough, so when they walked into the warehouse and ordered Moran's men to discard their weapons and line up against the back wall, the gangsters grumbled, but complied. They were expecting a little routine harassment. They got much more.

A few minutes after the "police" entered the warehouse, the neighborhood was assailed with the explosive crackling sound of machine-gun fire. When the bullets stopped, the two men in uniform exited the building with two captives, who looked suspiciously like the men who had accompanied them into the building. The ruse convinced bystanders that the cops had arrested the right people, and no one interfered as the fake cruiser sped away. When the sound of the roaring engine faded, the anguished howling of May's dog, Highball, could be heard.

The scene that was discovered inside the warehouse was horrifying. The seven men had been sprayed with bullets from two shotguns and two machine guns. In all, more than 150 rounds had been fired. One of the men, Frank Gusenberg, managed to drag his bullet-riddled body 20 feet from the gory scene. He lived long enough to be questioned by the police, who repeatedly asked him "Frank... who shot you?" Gusenberg's famous tough-guy retort was "Nobody shot me."

When it was all over, Bugs Moran fled Chicago. Al Capone had the city to himself once again, but he had paid a steep price. Opinion was turning against him, as people grew disgusted with the on-going bootleg wars. Following the massacre, Capone never knew another peaceful day—he was haunted until his death by the ghost of James Clark, Moran's brother-in-law (see "Chicago's Haunted Gangster," p. 27). Capone would not be allowed to forget his crime, nor the city of Chicago that dark day in its history.

When the old warehouse was torn down in 1967, 417 bricks from the rear wall were saved by a Canadian businessman named George Patey. Patey first built them into one wall of a Roaring Twenties nightclub he owned. After the club's demise, Patey salvaged the bricks once more, and concocted an even more tasteless money-making scheme. He sold the red blocks off individually, as macabre memorabilia of the famous massacre. Crime buffs were eager to buy the bullet-scarred bricks at $1000 apiece—but strangely, after a short time, many returned them to Patey. Few offered to explain why, but rumors began to circulate. It seemed that anyone who had purchased one of the old warehouse bricks was hit with a streak of terrible luck. Some became ill; some faced bankruptcy; still others were devastated by personal losses such as divorce, or a death in the family. The misfortunes were various, but all seemingly shared a common cause: disaster had struck immediately after the gruesome brick had been purchased. Probably many of the souvenirs were destroyed or discarded as the owners attempted to escape their powerful negative force. No one knows if any of the bricks remain intact today.

In fact, there is little physical evidence remaining to remind people of the dark and violent time when gangsters ruled Chicago's streets. As officials worked earnestly to clean up the city's image, they destroyed all the landmarks that were associated with the gangster era. Many people who have walked down Clark Street will tell you, however, that it's not that simple to erase the past.

The lot where the S-M-C Garage once stood is now the front lawn of a nursing home. This green space should be quiet and peaceful, but people have frequently reported hearing tormented screams or dreadful moans coming from the area. Dogs bristle and yelp when passing the lot, and some bark uncontrollably as if at an unseen threat. Perhaps they're joining Highball's howling lament for his murdered master.

And so the memories from that morning—and very possibly the spirits—remain to haunt Clark Street. Capone may have delivered his bloody Valentine more than 70 years ago, but it will take longer than that, and more than the destruction of a building, to eliminate the impression of violence and doom.

Chicago's Haunted Gangster

It is a known fact that, between 1920 and 1933, more than 700 gangland murders occurred in the Chicago area. What can only be estimated is how many of those killings were committed at the direct request of Alphonse "Scarface" Capone, the most powerful criminal spawned by that bloody era.

Capone's syndicate owned the City of Chicago, specializing in the lucrative businesses of bootlegging, gambling and prostitution. To protect the reported annual income of $100 million that his businesses provided, the country's most famous crime boss killed frequently, and without remorse. By some estimates, Al Capone may have been responsible for as many as 500 murders during his criminal career. Now, surely, a man like that can't be resting in peace?

There is a weak legend suggesting that Capone appears at his grave site to frighten disrespectful visitors. Another tale has it that a National Park Ranger once heard ghostly, residual strains of banjo music echoing in Capone's cell at Alcatraz. (The gangster played banjo in the prison band.) But apart from these rare accounts, there is nothing to suggest that the notorious criminal's tortured soul walks the earth. A yacht that Capone once owned— the *Duchess III*—appears to be haunted, but none of the spirits can be identified as the infamous Scarface. Below deck, in the bow of the boat, the apparition of a woman enduring a difficult childbirth can often be seen. Occasionally, in the same room, a concentrated mass of cold air has been known to wrap itself around visitors like an icy blanket. There are also reports of spectral lights moving from port hole to port hole through the empty yacht, but no sightings of the boat's unscrupulous one-time owner.

Although Al Capone hasn't put in much of an appearance as a ghost, a specter regularly appeared to him. For the last 18 years of his short life, he was haunted by the ghost of James Clark.

Clark was the brother-in-law of Capone's archrival, Bugs Moran, and one of Capone's victims in the ruthless St. Valentine's Day Massacre. When Capone masterminded the hit to rid himself of his enemies, he could not have known that Clark would exact revenge by haunting him to his own grave. In the years following the massacre, Capone's bodyguards and servants would often overhear him begging to be left alone. They would burst into the room, expecting to confront an intruder, and would find their boss alone. Every time, Capone would explain that he had been pleading with the specter of James Clark.

By 1931, Capone was so tormented by the ghost that he sought the help of a psychic named Alice Britt. Britt tried, but could not keep Clark's spirit from torturing Capone. The dead man's apparition continued to harass his murderer for 16 more years; through the gangster's conviction for income tax evasion, through his nearly eight years in prison, and through his mental and physical decline as a result of the syphilis he had contracted in his youth. When Al Capone finally died in Florida in 1947, some said it was James Clark, and not the disease, which had driven him mad.

In Chicago's Mount Carmel Cemetery, the stone that marks Capone's grave is surprisingly nondescript:

ALPHONSE CAPONE
1899–1947
MY JESUS MERCY

Perhaps that request for mercy has been granted, and Al Capone is finally resting in peace.

Haunted Dug Hill

A few miles west of Jonesboro, in Union County, is a mysterious place named Dug Hill. A road cut through this hill to allow easier passage to the Mississippi River hasn't much of a chilling effect today. But more than one century ago it was a dark, shadowy, dangerous stretch. It was also famous—as one of the most haunted spots in the southwest of Illinois.

In the 1800s, a late-night traveler, passing through the cut in the hill, came upon a gruesome discovery. There, in the middle of the rough, rutted road, was the body of a man. He was obviously unconscious, possibly even dead, and was lying face-down in a dark and spreading pool of blood. The traveler brought his horses to a halt, climbed down off his wagon, and rushed to the injured man's side. His first instinct was to turn the fellow over, so he reached down to get a firm grasp on the man's shoulder and hip.

His fingers dug into nothing more than dry dirt.

The traveler was flabbergasted, and stumbled back in shock. The body still lay on the road, and the blood still glistened in the moonlight. What seemed to have happened was impossible, so the traveler shook himself and tried, once more, to lift the body. This time, he watched with horror as his hands simply passed through the solid-looking form. Suddenly it seemed very wise to leave.

The traveler scrambled back up to the driver's seat and snapped the reins. The horses charged forward, and there was a sickening thud as the wagon's wooden wheels rolled over the body in the road. Questioning his sanity, the traveler turned for one look back. There was nothing on the road. Nothing at all.

The unlucky traveler had encountered the ghost of Dug Hill, the oft-seen specter of a Union Army provost marshal named Welch. Many came across Welch as a bleeding corpse; others claimed to have seen him staggering along the road in blood-soaked clothing, begging for help. The story of his death is an interesting one, for Welch could well be called a victim of the end of the Civil War.

As a provost marshal, one of Welch's duties was to round up deserters. Early in 1865, he arrested three such men, and had them imprisoned in Jonesboro. One day later, however, the signing of the peace treaty in Virginia ended the war—and the prisoners were released. The three renegades were free, but still seething, and decided to go looking for the man who had turned them in.

Near a dark curve on Dug Hill Road, the men concealed themselves and waited in ambush for the marshal. When Welch appeared, they jumped out with their pistols blazing. The provost marshal was shot to death and left in the road. His murderers were never captured. Soon after, Welch's restless spirit began to haunt that road, and people often reported hearing mysterious gunshots and the ghostly pounding of horse's hooves.

Occasionally, the hoof beats were accompanied by an apparition. People who were forced to stop along Dug Hill Road to repair a wagon wheel or, in later years, to fix a flat tire, sometimes reported being startled by the clamor of a team and wagon approaching at break-neck speed. The reports seldom varied. The rig would roar into sight and a collision would seem imminent, yet the two jet-colored horses would continue to charge ahead, with their heavy wooden cart clattering behind. Just before hitting the terrified travelers, the transport would thunder into the air above them, the horse's hooves and wagon wheels battering and grinding, respectively, against nothing more than the cool, night air. The vision would then sail into the distance, out of sight and hearing.

The driver of the runaway rig has never been identified—but there are those who think it might be Provost Marshal Welch, making one last attempt to escape the fate he met on that dark night at Dug Hill.

The Hull House Devil Baby

It could be said that Chicago has a history of dealing with the Devil. The city has the dubious honor of being the birthplace of Anton LaVey, who would later go on to found and lead the Church of Satan. There is a decades-old tale in the neighborhood of Bridgeport about a charming stranger who once spent an evening dazzling a lonely young woman at a local dance hall—until she glanced down and, with horror and revulsion, noticed his cloven feet. And then, of course, there is the story of the Hull House Devil Baby.

Hull House was built in 1856 as the private residence of a wealthy real estate man named Charles Hull. Hull lived there for only a dozen years. Within another dozen years, the mansion had become surrounded by factories and tenement housing. The surroundings were quite undesirable to anyone who could afford to live in such a grand home, but perfectly suitable for the purposes of a social worker named Jane Addams. With a woman named Ellen Gates Starr, Addams rented Hull House in 1889 and turned it into a center for good works. Addams and Starr fed the hungry, clothed the poor, sheltered the homeless and provided comfort and hope to every needy person who walked through their door. Hull House was a pioneering effort in the war against poverty, providing assistance that was available nowhere else to Chicago's large community of new immigrants. As demand increased and new programs were developed, more space was required. A third floor was added to the house, and eventually 12 additional structures were erected around the original building, forming a

By 1918, Hull House was nearly obscured by other buildings in the complex. Shown here (left to right) are the Butler Art Gallery, Hull House and the Children's Building (the Smith Building).

complex that housed schools, clubs, the neighborhood's only library, and one of the first gymnasiums in the country.

Although the foundation of Hull House was considered to be an unprecedented achievement—the building itself was designated a historic landmark in June 1967, and Jane Addams would receive a Nobel Prize for her charitable work—the place is best known for a bizarre rumor that spread like wildfire through the city during six strange weeks in the spring of 1913.

Hull House, people whispered, was housing the child of Satan.

In those few weeks, when the story was at its apex, hundreds made the journey to speak with Addams and her staff, begging for a glimpse of the famous "Devil Baby."

Those who made the trek knew in detail what they had come to see: the Devil Baby was a horned child with cloven hooves and a short, pointed tail. The baby spoke from the moment of its birth, people insisted—in fact, its first act was to dance merrily around the room cursing its terrified parents. The monster even smoked a cigar, according to some, and had been seen driving about the city in a red automobile. When efforts to baptize and tame the infant failed, the distraught parents brought it to Hull House, where Jane Addams kept it locked away in an upstairs room.

The story baffled and disgusted Addams, who was, nonetheless, intrigued by its intense detail. There was even a tale about how the imp had come to be—a tale that varied slightly, from one ethnic group to the next.

In Chicago's Irish community, the story went that a young girl married without confessing to her priest that she had been with another man before her husband. For this offense, she was forced to give birth to the Devil. Among the Italians, it was said that a woman married an atheist, against the wishes of her family. When she became pregnant with their first child, she tried to hang a picture of the Blessed Virgin on the wall, but her husband threw it into the fire, declaring that he would rather have the Devil in his house than a holy picture. His invitation was accepted and the monstrous child was born. There were a number of Jewish versions of the story, including one in which a Jewish girl married a gentile, causing her father furiously to shout, "I would rather have the Devil as a grandchild than a gentile as a son-in-law!" In another version, a pregnant woman lied to her rabbi, claiming to be having her first child, when in fact she had given birth to one out of wedlock. All stories in all cultures were the same, however, in that they offered a serious lesson: it was a sin to stray from one's culture, one's family or one's religion. To do so would result in dire consequences.

What united the tales was a theme of morality; what united the pilgrims to Hull House was their station in life. Nearly all the visitors who requested to see the Devil Baby were older, isolated, immigrant women. These matrons rarely ventured beyond the neighborhood church or market, but were doing everything in their limited power to pay a visit to the Devil Baby. Sociologist and author Dr. Barrie Robinson speculates that their visits were to be expected, given the nature of the tale and the position of the women.

According to Robinson's theory, these matriarchs of European families were the traditional "keepers of the ways." They spent their days instructing the young in the ways of the old, and often issued warnings of the dire consequences that would befall those who strayed from the proper path. Given their role in the communities, it is little wonder that these women were among the first to venture out to see the legendary Devil Baby: the child was a confirmation of what they had spent their lives preaching.

Jane Addams herself grew more patient with the visits as time went on, and took to meeting and speaking personally with the older visitors. Through her interviews, she gained valuable insight into what motivated these women, and an appreciation for the effect that the story had on them. She would later write about it:

> During the weeks of excitement... it was the old women who really seemed to have come into their own, and perhaps the most significant result of the incident was the reaction of the story upon them. It stirred their minds and memory as with a magic touch, it loosened their tongues and revealed the inner life and thoughts of those who are so often inarticulate. They are accustomed to sit at home and to hear the younger members of the family speak of affairs quite outside their own experiences in a language they do not understand.

Wisely, Addams took the strange opportunity to educate the public about the drab and sequestered nature of these women's lives. According to author Ursula Bielski in *Chicago Haunts: Ghostlore of the Windy City* (1998), "Addams peered into the myth with a keenly interpretive eye and revealed it as a complex expression of cultural concerns." What she did not seem to ponder, Dr. Barrie Robinson pointed out many years later, is why her establishment was singled out for peculiar attention among the older women. He filled in her theory with some observations of his own.

In the early 20th century, the United States was still heavily influenced by Social Darwinism. There were many who strongly believed that society's unfortunates should be left on their own to survive or perish, and that interfering with this natural selection was interfering with both God and Nature. Hull House, as a place of charity, flew in the face of these long-standing beliefs in self-reliance. According to Robinson, it was an easy target for rumor and suspicion. People had no idea what transpired within those walls, and they weren't about to imagine something mundane.

Generations later, however, in a time when social programs are the norm and Hull House has been preserved as a museum, storytellers are keeping the Devil Baby alive in the only way they can—as a ghost story. The museum is a favorite stop for ghost hunters, who will pause outside and peer at the upstairs windows. Some say that an evil little face can occasionally be seen looking out at the street below. Other tales tell of shadowy figures and ectoplasmic mists that appear on the inside staircase—phenomena which are sometimes attributed to a suicide which is rumored (but was never proven) to have taken place in one of the upstairs rooms.

Despite the persistence of the ghost stories, there are few today who truly believe that there ever was a Hull House Devil Baby. The closest that anyone comes, in theory, is to suggest that there may have once been a deformed child taken in by the House and hidden away from prying eyes.

If anyone sees fit to haunt this historic place, it might be the spirit of Jane Addams. She devoted her life to the poor, but will always be remembered as the keeper of the infamous Devil Baby.

The Sorrow of Angels

In Queen of Heaven Cemetery, in the Chicago suburb of Hillside, stands a breathtaking memorial to children who perished in a fire. The fire occurred at Our Lady of the Angels School and is considered to be one of the greatest tragedies in Chicago in the last 50 years. It happened in December 1958, and took the lives of 92 children and three nuns.

The fire is believed to have started in a trash can at the bottom of a basement stairwell. Within minutes, the flames were rapidly licking across the steps and walls, meeting nothing but flammable surfaces. By the time the first fire engine arrived—it was initially sent to the wrong address, and then was unable to enter the courtyard of the school because of a locked gate—the entire upper floor of the north wing was burning. The wooden parish school was filled with flames, black smoke, unbearable heat—and children. The firefighters worked heroically. They rescued 160 terrified students, but there was much they could not do. In the end, 95 victims died in the fire. The public cried out with grief and rage.

The sad truth is that the fire was able to claim so many lives only because safety regulations of the day were lax. Our Lady of the Angels had no smoke detectors, no sprinkler systems and no fire doors at the top of the second-floor staircases. There was only one fire escape, and the window ledges were too high for many of the children to climb over. The single fire alarm rang only inside the building, and thus provided no alert to the neighborhood or the local fire department. Legally, however, there was no problem.

The school had passed a safety inspection only two months before the blaze.

The fire caused overwhelming sorrow. Thankfully, it also resulted in amendments to fire safety codes for schools across the country. Thirdly, it gave rise to a number of unforgettable stories. Most involve mysterious premonitions and unexpected consolation in the days surrounding the tragedy.

One mother had the startling vision of her small son in a casket on the evening before the fire. There were likely countless others who shrugged off uncomfortable feelings and seemingly inexplicable anxieties in the hours leading up to the disaster.

Following the inferno, some families that had lost children reported being comforted by their spirits. "Don't worry," one little ghost assured her anguished brother, "I'm going to watch over you." Similar consolation was provided by the apparition of a little boy, who sat with his mother and held her hand after she had been to the morgue to identify his body.

There were also reports of "crisis apparitions"—ghosts that appear to loved ones at a time of crisis or death. One of the most heart-wrenching was the story of a boy who searched frantically for his sister in the chaotic scene outside the burning school. Relief washed over him when he saw the little girl walking off in the direction of their home. When he returned home himself, however, he learned that his sister had perished in the blaze.

There are other ghost stories concerning the fire at Our Lady of the Angels, but none that bear repeating. Even after more than 40 years, the painful nature of this event requires that only the most sensitive and respectful tales be told. Perhaps in another 40 years, the situation will bear a more analytical eye, but for now it is important to let these angels rest.

Dillinger's Last Show

"Look under your bed!"

"Search your cellar!"

"Dillinger is hiding somewhere here. And he may be hiding in your backyard!"

In the spring of 1934, the city of Chicago was caught up in a frenzy over the whereabouts of one man—Public Enemy Number One, John Dillinger. Within a few short months, Dillinger had become a notorious gangster and dark folk hero, wanted for a number of robberies, two prison breaks and murder. Now he was believed to be hiding out on Chicago's North Side, and the excitement was unparalleled.

Dillinger's exploits made fantastic copy for the newspapers of the day. He was well-dressed, photogenic and possessed of the sort of flash and charm that made the public swoon. He stole from banks—which, in the Depression, were hated for their failures and foreclosures—and delighted in making the police and FBI look like buffoons. His gutsy antics made him popular, but there was a considerable price on his head by that warm spring of 1934, and the gangster wasn't counting on any loyalty from the public.

Dillinger found a doctor willing to alter his face surgically. Three moles and a scar were removed, and the cleft of his chin and the bridge of his nose were filled in. The famous criminal then resolved to lay low, look for one more big score, and then escape to Mexico with the loot. He had a hunch that his luck was about to run out—he just didn't know how soon.

The gangster was hiding out with his new girlfriend, a 26-year-old waitress named Polly Hamilton. He had given her a false name and told her that he worked for the Chicago Board of Trade. Hamilton either didn't question the story or didn't care; her new paramour had given her a diamond ring and enough cash to allow her to have her teeth fixed. She was happy.

Polly Hamilton had a friend named Anna Sage who was much less credulous. Spending more and more time with the happy couple, she became convinced that Polly's boyfriend "Jimmy" was in fact the notorious John Dillinger. Because Sage was facing a few legal problems of her own—the greatest of them was deportation to Romania—a fistful of reward money and a little bargaining power with the FBI seemed very attractive. The woman contacted the authorities and informed them that she could deliver the elusive Dillinger.

On July 22, 1934, Anna Sage, Polly Hamilton and John Dillinger went out to watch a film at the Biograph Theater on north Lincoln Avenue. Sage wore a bright red dress which made her easy to spot in the crowd of moviegoers. There was a reason for her choice of clothing: as the trio entered the Biograph, they were carefully watched by 16 members of the FBI and Chicago Police. Dillinger enjoyed the show. He had no idea that he had been identified, and that a trap awaited him. The audience members, watching the gangster flick *Manhattan Melodrama*, had no idea that they were about to see some real cops and robbers in action.

At around 10:30 PM, the movie let out and the crowd began to emerge from the theater. Dillinger and his lady friends stepped out onto the sidewalk, and the FBI's careful plan was set in motion. Melvin Purvis, the head of the Chicago FBI, positively identified Dillinger, and signaled the others to close the net.

Dillinger had looked directly at Purvis, and may have recognized him, for after a few more steps, he suddenly bolted down a narrow alley. The agents, who had been repeatedly embarrassed by Dillinger's escapes, needed no greater excuse: four shots were fired at the fleeing criminal. They met their mark. Dillinger crashed to the ground. Public Enemy Number One was dead.

The sensation surrounding Dillinger's death was even greater than that caused by his life, and it began immediately. As soon as the frantic crowd learned the identity of the dead man, it swarmed forward to see the body. Some people dipped handkerchiefs and pieces of newspaper in the pool of blood, creating macabre souvenirs to take home. Others simply gaped in amazement.

Newspapers rushed to turn out extra editions. Within hours, the bar next door to the Biograph Theater hung out a large, hand-painted sign that proclaimed, "DILLINGER HAD HIS LAST DRINK HERE." And at the Cook County morgue, the scene was unreal. Hundreds of curious people lined up to view Dillinger's corpse. Even the coroner was caught up in the carnival-like atmosphere, and posed cheerfully with the body for a number of photographs.

Some onlookers found the experience less exciting than they had imagined. "I'm disappointed," one woman was quoted as saying. "Looks just like any other dead man." And, in fact, there were those who were saying that it was some other dead man, and not John Dillinger at all.

Disbelief that Dillinger had been killed likely stemmed from the fact that he had made a reputation for himself as the slipperiest of escape artists. Doubt regarding his identity might have been a result of his surgically altered features. Some reports insist that the dead man did not match Dillinger's description, recording that the corpse had brown eyes, whereas Dillinger's were blue; that the man shot and killed was inches shorter and pounds heavier than Dillinger; and that the corpse showed a rheumatic heart condition which was not listed on John Dillinger's naval service records. On the same night Dillinger was killed, a small-time hood named Jimmy Lawrence disappeared. Many believe that it was he who lay displayed on a slab in the Cook County morgue for all of Chicago to see.

Whether it was Dillinger or an unwitting stand-in who took the bullets in the back that night, the spirit of the killed man seems uneasy. Approximately 40 years after the fatal shoot-out, pedestrians on Lincoln Avenue began to see some strange things. Glancing down what had become known as "Dillinger's Alley," they could sometimes spot a shadowy blue figure running, stumbling and disappearing upon contact with the ground. Some people reported walking into a shocking wall of cold air, or sensing another presence on the exact site of the gangster's death. Reportedly, the experiences had in the alley are so unpleasant that locals no longer use it as a short cut to Halsted Street.

Naturally, ghost hunters, tourists and crime buffs do not shy away from entering the alley. Most of them take away a splinter of wood from a utility pole that sits inches away from the spot where Dillinger died, as a souvenir of their visit. What few know is that the pole is not the original. It has been replaced twice since that night in 1934. It seems that the two previous poles were picked to bits by earlier souvenir hunters.

John Dillinger may be gone, but his mystique lives on. There remains great interest in the life, death and now the afterlife of the gangster once named Public Enemy Number One.

The Watseka Wonder

Lurancy Vennum was a happy, well-adjusted, 13-year-old girl who lived with her parents in the sleepy town of Watseka, 50 miles south of Chicago. Mary Roff, whose parents also lived in Watseka, was a seemingly disturbed teenager who had died in a mental hospital when Lurancy was only a baby. In January 1878, these two girls who had never known one another each played a part in a bizarre situation that over one century later still stands as one of the best-documented and most convincing cases of spirit possession on record.

In July 1877, young Lurancy began having catatonic spells, during which she claimed to have traveled to heaven and spoken with spirits. The girl's trances could occur as often as a dozen times a day, and sometimes last as long as eight hours.

In January 1878, the distraught Vennums agreed to let Dr. E. Winchester Stevens, a spiritualist physician, examine their daughter. Dr. Stevens confirmed that Lurancy was possessed by a number of undesirable spirits, and not mentally ill as most people believed. He suggested to the girl that she allow one friendly spirit to take over her body, until she herself was strong enough to reassume control. The friendly spirit that moved in was Mary Roff.

Once Mary Roff was present, Lurancy Vennum seemed to disappear completely. She was polite to her parents, but clearly uncomfortable with them, and repeatedly requested that she be allowed "to go home." Finally, in February 1878, the Vennums arranged to have their daughter stay with the Roffs, despite the limited acquaintance of the families. The girl seemed delighted at seeing her "real family" once more, and for the next three months became their child.

During that time, the Roffs were continually amazed at how familiar Lurancy-as-Mary was with the minute details of their lives. She called people by nicknames that few others knew; she had a flawless knowledge of the family history, including events that happened prior to the Roffs' move to Watseka; and she identified old personal objects and answered hundreds of questions without fault. She was openly affectionate with each of the Roffs and their family friends, recalling the most intimate moments of relationships that had been established long before Lurancy's birth. And every time the Roffs set out to test their "daughter," she passed with flying colors.

On one occasion, Mrs. Roff found a velvet hair ornament that had belonged to Mary. She set it out on a small table and said nothing. When Lurancy walked in the room, she recognized it immediately, and exclaimed, "Oh, there is my headdress I wore when my hair was short!" In other instances, the girl identified a collar she had tatted, pointed to the exact spot where the family dog had died, and recalled a number of specific details about a move to Texas that the Roffs had made in 1857. Mr. and Mrs. Roff were thoroughly convinced that in the body of Lurancy Vennum lived the memories, personality, and spirit of their long-lost Mary.

They were equally convinced that Mary had never been insane, but had suffered from a case of spirit possession similar to Lurancy's.

In May 1878, Mary announced tearfully to the Roffs that it was time for her to leave: the angels wanted her back in heaven, and Lurancy's own spirit was now well enough to resume control of her body. Good-byes were said, and Lurancy's consciousness resurfaced. The girl looked anxiously around the room and asked,

"Where am I?" The strange situation was explained to her. Lurancy burst into tears and announced that she wanted to go home.

Lurancy Vennum did go home, and was cured of her catatonic spells from that day on. Although she remembered little of her ordeal, she maintained a friendship with the Roff family and felt a tremendous gratitude toward Mary Roff, whom she believed to be her savior. As a show of appreciation, Lurancy, whenever she visited the Roffs, would allow Mary to enter her body and speak with her parents. It was a strange arrangement that continued for many years, until Lurancy moved to Kansas with her husband.

Skeptics of the day found the account of Lurancy-as-Mary a difficult case to disprove. It was once described as "undoubtedly the best possession case on record, answering as it does most of the intelligent arguments that could be raised against it." Lurancy Vennum and Mary Roff made their marks on both the history of Illinois, and the history of paranormal research, when they came together to create a wonder in Watseka.

Chapter 2

GHOST RIDERS

*The most popular paranormal tales, particularly
in North America given our fascination with cars, are
likely those involving phantom hitchhikers. Stories
of these eternally wandering spirits touch on all the
elements of fantasy, including the lonely traveler,
the mysterious young woman, the danger and
romance of a dark (and often stormy) night,
and the endless possibilities of the open road.
It is hardly surprising that such irresistible tales
have been around since time immemorial.*

*Some variations on this theme of phantom
hitchhikers have included phantom vehicles,
which seem intent upon forcing terrified motorists
off the road, and spectral jaywalkers, who stand in
the path of oncoming cars, waiting to be run down.
The unlucky drivers will see the "victim" at the
last moment, and often feel the sickening thud
of impact. When they search for a body,
however, they can find none.*

*If you are prepared for a trip into the unknown—
complete with a few unwanted
passengers—read on.*

Resurrection Mary

In the ghost lore of Illinois, there is one tale that stands out among the rest—a tale famous for its drama and endurance. It is the story of Resurrection Mary, the beautiful phantom hitchhiker who makes her home in the Chicago suburb of Justice, Illinois.

For nearly seven decades, people have delighted in telling Mary's story. She has been on television and in print, and is even the subject of a song. Encounters with her are frequent, by ghost story standards, and each witness is eager to add his or her experience to the growing collection of tales. But curiously, despite the many encounters, Resurrection Mary remains somewhat elusive, in the investigative sense.

Nailing down her nature has proven impossible. Determined efforts to link her spirit to a once-real person have resulted in questionable connections, at best. Even as a legend, she stubbornly defies being categorized, choosing one day to act the part of the classic "vanishing hitchhiker" and another day to fill the role of the "spectral jaywalker." Just when you think you have her pegged as an urban legend, she makes a convincing appearance. There is truly no other Illinois ghost that intrigues, frustrates and delights in equal measure with Resurrection Mary.

It all began in 1936.

A young man named Jerry Palus was treating himself to a night on the town. He was out to meet the ladies, and he found a lovely one at the Liberty Grove Hall and Ballroom, then a popular spot on Chicago's Southwest Side.

She was a breathtaking blonde with light blue eyes, dressed elegantly in a snowy white cocktail dress with matching satin dancing shoes. Palus was taken with her beauty but somewhat puzzled by her aloof nature: although she danced with him throughout the evening, he would later describe her as being rather distant and cold. And she was cold in more than the emotional sense, for when she granted Palus a goodnight kiss, he was surprised by the clammy touch of her lips.

As the band played its last song, Palus offered his dancing partner a ride home. She accepted, and directed him to drive along Archer Avenue. As the car neared the gates of Resurrection Cemetery, she told him to pull over. The girl then turned to Palus and explained that she had to leave, and that he could not follow her. Palus was confused as he watched her walk away from the safety of his car in what was a deserted and remote area. It's a guarantee that he was more than just confused after what happened next. He saw his date for the evening melt through the high iron gates of the cemetery, then vanish from sight on the other side.

This was the first of many sightings of Resurrection Mary. For Jerry Palus, it was an experience so profound that he would spend the rest of his life recounting it to anyone who would listen.

In 1939, the police began registering complaints from late-night motorists along Archer Avenue. They told of a strange woman who would try to jump on the running boards of their cars as they drove by. There was nothing in particular to link her to Jerry Palus's frigid date—but that is not to say she wasn't the same girl. Resurrection Mary may have simply been establishing what would become a decades-long habit of inconsistent behavior.

For example, although Mary's first documented date was at the Liberty Grove Hall and Ballroom, there are no subsequent reports of her returning there. Over the years, she became closely associated with the Oh Henry Ballroom (later renamed the Willowbrook). She surfaced there so often that people were sure she must have died traveling to or from that location.

During the glitter-rock craze of the 1970s, Mary ventured out to another club, called Harlow's, on South Cicero Avenue in

Chicago. She must have liked it—the manager at the time claimed to have seen her twice within the span of one month. The girl stood out, he said, because of her strange, outdated appearance and isolated manner. She refused to speak to anyone and seemed oblivious to those around her. She spent both evenings dancing alone, performing odd pirouettes around the couples on the dance floor. But most mysterious of all was that no one saw her enter or exit the club. Staff were posted at all doors, and it was Harlow's policy to see identification from every patron, yet no one remembered admitting the very distinctive-looking girl. The manager found no solution to the puzzle until several years later, when he read a newspaper article describing Resurrection Mary in all her pale, blonde glory.

Despite the precise description in such articles, Resurrection Mary's appearance—and hence her origin—is still hotly contested. The most popular theory is that she is the ghost of a young woman, likely of Polish descent, named Mary Bregovy, who died in an automobile accident in March 1934 while traveling home from the Oh Henry Ballroom. But as pervasive as this explanation is, it's an ill-fitting shoe: Bregovy had short, dark hair, quite unlike the long, fair, ringlets of the vanishing spirit. Bregovy was buried in an orchid-colored dress, rather than white lace. Furthermore, the scene of her accidental death was downtown Chicago—nowhere near the Oh Henry or Archer Avenue.

Some researchers have claimed that the real-life Mary was a 12-year-old girl named Ona Norkus, who died in a car accident after an evening at the Oh Henry Ballroom with her father (see "The Sneering Specter of St. Casimir," page 57). Foiling this theory is the assertion by Mary's dancing partners that she is much more than 12. Besides, Ona Norkus had little to do with Resurrection Cemetery, which Resurrection Mary quite obviously regards as home.

Truly, the one consistency in Resurrection Mary's otherwise erratic behavior is her association with the cemetery for which she is named. Every time she ventures out dancing, she requests a ride home along Archer Avenue, and disappears at exactly the same location, in front of the forbidding iron gates. Every time an unsuspecting driver stops to offer a lift to a young, blonde hitchhiker who later vanishes, it happens close to the cemetery. Some might even say Mary loves Resurrection Cemetery so much that she once left her physical mark on it.

Late one night in the mid-1970s, a lone young woman in a fancy white dress was spotted wandering around behind the locked cemetery gates. As the passing motorist saw her, she stepped forward and grabbed the iron bars with her fists, as if to shake the gates in an effort to escape. The driver thought it obvious that someone had been locked inside Resurrection Cemetery after closing time, and stopped at the first police station to ask for assistance on the woman's behalf.

The police sergeant who was dispatched to the scene found the cemetery empty, and the gates bearing an intriguing piece of evidence. Two of the heavy metal bars had been pried apart. Where they had been gripped, there remained the distinct impressions of two dainty handprints, seared into the iron.

What happened next is difficult to know. According to some reports, the cemetery management immediately reported the bars to the Archbishop of Chicago, who had the affected portions removed for study. Others say that the offending segments were repaired—and, indeed, there are very distinct discolorations on the two bars, to this day.

Still others say that the entire incident can be easily explained away. They say that one of the cemetery's groundskeepers accidentally backed into the gate with his truck, bending the bars out of shape. He and his co-workers allegedly then tried to fix the situation by heating the metal with a blowtorch, and forcing the bars back into place. The plan didn't work, but the imprints of one man's work gloves were left in the hot iron.

All this speculation introduces another group of players in the story of Resurrection Mary: the non-believers. As adamant as those who believe in this winsome spirit are those who do not. One man with years of experience maintaining the huge Resurrection Mausoleum claimed never to have witnessed anything strange or mysterious. He often had to patrol the grounds on Halloween, and even slept in the mausoleum one night when a storm prevented him from getting home. Still, he insisted that nothing untoward happened at Resurrection Cemetery—and many local citizens agree with him.

There are lifelong residents of Justice who have never seen Mary, don't believe the stories and don't like the way the myth attracts gawking tourists to their otherwise quiet community. One Halloween, a local woman named Ausra Kiela thought she would poke a bit of fun at all the out-of-towners by dressing up as the famous Mary and strolling along Archer Avenue by the cemetery. She desisted when she found that drivers were taking her very seriously, stopping their cars and offering her rides.

Among the more open-minded in Justice are the people who own and operate Chet's Melody Lounge, a bar located across the street and down from Resurrection Cemetery. It is a favorite hangout for Mary-watchers and the first place shaken drivers stop after an unexpected encounter with the spirit. Recent sightings are rare, but the owners offer a number of intriguing stories from years gone by.

In 1973, an angry cab driver burst into the lounge, demanding, "Where's the blonde?" He was looking for a young woman in a white dress who had soundlessly disappeared from the back seat of his cab, just moments earlier, in the parking lot. The bar was the only place she could be. The driver wanted his fare, so everyone helped search the lounge and ladies' room but, of course, the girl was never found.

On other occasions—and as recently as 1996—someone would run into Chet's Melody Lounge begging for help, claiming to have accidentally run down a woman in a white dress who was walking along Archer Avenue. The worst shock for these drivers was that when they got out of their vehicles and approached the woman, her broken, bloodied body would vanish before their eyes. Other motorists—those fortunate enough to have one of the less grisly versions of the experience—would report that the woman in white would either vanish the instant she was hit, or pass through the engine compartment of the vehicle and then run off toward the cemetery.

Was it Mary? If so, these stories lend support to yet another theory regarding her identity and demise. Perhaps she was the ghost of a girl who had been struck by a car and killed after deciding to walk home from the Oh Henry Ballroom after a fight with her boyfriend.

Although the various theories differ widely, they agree on one point: it would seem that men—whether boyfriends, fathers or drivers—were responsible for the original Mary's undoing. Could that be why Resurrection Mary chooses to materialize primarily to men?

One night, two friends named Kristin and Susan decided to force a meeting with the famous apparition. They spent some time at Chet's Melody Lounge, playing pool and plugging the jukebox to hear "The Ballad of Resurrection Mary." At 2 AM, they left, driving the short distance up Archer Avenue to the cemetery. There they parked, got out of the car, walked up to the gates to examine the scorched segments on the bars, and peered beyond them into the shadowy darkness. They didn't see any mysterious young women in filmy white gowns, but they had given themselves a good case of the willies and decided it was time to leave.

Kristin was driving, and dropped her friend off before heading to her own home. When she arrived, her boyfriend met her at the door, looking puzzled. "Where's Susan?" he asked. Kristin explained that she had taken Susan home several minutes earlier. "Then who was in the car with you?" was his next question. Kristin's blood ran cold. To this day, her boyfriend insists that when he looked out the window at the approaching car, he saw Kristin sitting in the driver's seat, and the figure of another woman sitting beside her. Though she had been in the car with Kristin, Resurrection Mary, it seemed, remained an exclusively male vision.

There are a number of stories which prove that Mary likes to deviate from her regular pattern. One Christmas season in the late 1980s, she was spotted, not hitchhiking, but dancing in a bizarre fashion on the road outside the cemetery gates. She pranced about, wearing nothing more than a party dress and satin slippers, though it was the middle of December. The young men who witnessed it were most spooked because only they seemed to see her. Several other passers-by appeared oblivious to the spectral show.

By January 1989, Mary had returned to hitchhiking, but seemed confused and unsure of herself. In one of the most famous of all Mary sightings, a cab driver picked her up outside the Old Willow Shopping Center. The night was stormy and freezing cold, but the girl, of course, was clad in her usual attire. On this occasion, she sat in the front of the cab, and vaguely indicated that the driver should proceed up Archer Avenue. She made very little conversation and even less sense. In response to the driver's polite attempts at small talk, she offered only one reasonably clear statement: "The snow came early this year." Those few words seemed to rob her of all her energy. She said nothing more until the cab came to the main gates of Resurrection Cemetery. Then she yelled out

"Here!" and disappeared through the car door, without bothering to open it. The shocked driver watched his passenger run into a weathered shed that sat directly across the road from the cemetery entrance.

Many attribute the ghost's restlessness in the 1970s and disorientation in the 1980s to a renovation of Resurrection Cemetery that took place over several years. It is quite likely that Mary was buried sometime in the early 1930s, and she may have been in what was called a "term grave." These plots were sold on 25-year terms, then made available to the families for repurchase. If no one came forward to buy a second lease for Mary's grave site, it may eventually have been used again. That would indeed be enough to bewilder a spirit. Imagine—you go out dancing one night, and return to find someone else in your eternal resting spot.

All of these stories of Resurrection Mary—from the dance with Jerry Palus through the phantom accidents to the cab ride from the Old Willow Shopping Center—make her a difficult ghost to classify. Stories of vanishing hitchhikers abound in North American culture, and it is tempting to isolate some elements of Mary's behavior and categorize her as one. She refuses, however, to be so tidily pigeon-holed. To begin with, Mary talks more than the average phantom hitchhiker of legend. Moreover, she often couples hitchhiking with a night out: not always content with a brief car ride, she has spent numerous evenings at numerous dances with numerous young men.

Sociologist and author Dr. Barrie Robinson makes the case for Mary's being an urban legend. Urban legends tend to serve as cautionary tales, and Resurrection Mary might just have a lesson hidden behind all her sensational behavior. Having read a number of stories about Mary, Robinson suggests that the ghost story may have initially served as a morality tale for people of central and east European descent in Chicago.

These conservative and predominantly Roman Catholic people would have found a comforting affirmation of their strict moral code in the story of Resurrection Mary. Mary's fate was proof of the dangers that were said to befall any young girl who engaged in such unacceptable activities as dancing, drinking and consorting with men. Robinson points to the physical description of Mary as evidence: with her virginal dress and blonde, angelic appearance, she fits the stereotype of the good girl gone wrong. Mary stepped outside the moral boundaries defined by the community, and is paying the price for all eternity.

But if the story of Resurrection Mary is a morality tale, how does one account for the growing popularity of Mary's story in recent decades, which have been socially and morally less restrictive? Robinson addresses this question as well. The motivation behind a legend can change over time. Where morality was once essential for the propagation of the story, the desire for publicity and profit may now have taken root. Local businesses and tourist attractions could be exploiting the tale—as could those authors who write about it.

It is true that Resurrection Mary is the most often written-about ghost in the state. And Chet's Melody Lounge can probably thank her for a portion of its liquor sales over the years. Whether Resurrection Mary is the product of supernatural forces, traditional wisdom or the profit motive, one thing is clear: she is alive and well in the culture of Illinois.

Ask the incredulous people who have met her, over the years. Ask the kids who have made it a rite of passage to go searching for the spirit, upon receiving their first driver's license. Ask the bartender at Chet's. He routinely leaves a Bloody Mary on the end of the bar at closing time, just in case his famous neighbor drops by to slake her thirst.

The Sneering Specter of St. Casimir

In southwest Chicago is a well-kept Lithuanian cemetery named St. Casimir. It is home to a phantom whom no one wishes to encounter. He does no harm, he brings no bad luck, but his very appearance is so menacing that those who have had the misfortune to meet him have reported that the shock affected them for days.

When the ghost is described, one can understand why. He is a thin man, unkempt, with a sickly pallor. He alarms motorists who are driving by the cemetery by suddenly appearing in the beams of their headlights. The unappealing shade's face is distorted in an expression of utter malevolence—a sneer so hate-filled and focused that, no matter how fast the drivers slam on the brakes, terror hits them with the force of a head-on collision. For a long, horrible moment, the specter pins them with his baleful glare, and then he disappears, simply vanishing as suddenly as he appeared.

Recently, a story has emerged that would connect St. Casimir's unappealing wraith with the lovely and mysterious Resurrection Mary. In July 1927, a 12-year-old girl named Ona Norkus died in a car accident. Ona was with her father, August Norkus, who had accompanied her to the Oh Henry Ballroom for an evening of dancing. The night out was meant to be a gift for the girl's upcoming birthday. As it happened, she never would turn 13.

The Norkuses had a family plot at St. Casimir Cemetery. Since gravedigger strikes were common in the 1920s, little Ona's body may have been temporarily buried at Resurrection Cemetery, and never moved to its proper resting place. The speculation that follows is that the threatening presence who haunts the street by St. Casimir might actually be a distraught August Norkus, searching for his lost daughter.

This explanation overlooks two details, however: St. Casimir's ghost is in the business of intimidating, rather than seeking, and Resurrection Mary has clearly appeared, to her many witnesses, to be much older than 12. And so, as inviting as it may be to connect the two legends, the horrible specter of St. Casimir Cemetery remains a mystery.

The Stowaway

A man from the Decatur area bought a new pickup truck one spring. He was quite proud of his purchase. The truck was well equipped to handle any driving conditions, so negotiating the muddy backroads as the snow and ice melted became an enjoyable pastime.

One particularly fine afternoon, the man decided to indulge his interest in local history and visit a remote rural cemetery east of the city. He found the burial ground in distressing shape: frost heaves during the winter had been severe enough to upset several headstones, and the earth was soft with pools of water and mud.

The man parked his truck on one of the unpaved paths that wound through the cemetery, and began wandering about, letting the sparse information on the gravestones fire his imagination. After some time, the shadows began to lengthen and the man realized it was time to be leaving for home. He climbed back into the pickup and drove away.

About a mile beyond the cemetery gates, he happened to glance to his right. Unbelievably, in the passenger seat, there sat an old woman who had most certainly not been in the vehicle moments earlier. The man gasped with surprise and struggled to keep control of the steering wheel. He felt his skin go cold. With great effort, he forced himself to stare straight ahead for a few moments, concentrating on the road and his driving. When he felt it safe to do so, he risked a glance back at the passenger seat. The woman was still there.

She appeared ancient, with a wizened face and tidy silver hair. Her dress was light blue, with long sleeves and a conservative high collar. She sat still, staring forward, never turning to look at the driver and never moving her hands, which lay clasped together in her lap.

The man was gripped by indecision. Abandoning his truck on a deserted country road seemed unwise. Speaking to the ghost seemed ludicrous. He continued to drive. After several more uneasy miles, he risked another glance to his right. The woman, he discovered, had vanished.

Shaking with relief, the man pulled into the parking lot of the first bar he could find. He ordered a double to steady his nerves, and began to replay the experience in his mind. It was too bizarre to believe, and by the time he returned to his obviously empty truck with a few shots of whiskey under his belt, he had half-convinced himself that the old woman had been produced by his imagination. The man drove home, and did his best to put the whole episode out of his mind.

For a few days, that worked.

Then one afternoon, the man was driving home from work when he happened to glance over to the passenger seat. The old woman was there once again, sitting and staring straight ahead, exactly as before. This time the man hit the brakes, bringing his new truck to a dangerous and screeching stop at the side of the road. He jumped out and slammed the driver's door behind him.

In a country graveyard like this, a Decatur man unknowingly picked up an uninvited passenger.

Taking several deep breaths, he attempted to revive himself with the cold spring air. "She must be gone, she must be gone," he chanted to himself before turning to take another look. She was not. All things carefully considered, the man decided to walk.

After a few minutes, however, he questioned his judgment. In its precarious position on the side of the road, the new truck could easily be hit or, worse, stolen. And, as unnerving as she was, the ghost of the old woman had never threatened him in any way. Ignoring his sense of dread, the man reluctantly returned to the truck. It now sat mockingly empty, but this time the man did not question what he knew had happened.

Six months later, the old woman appeared one last time, and then disappeared for good. Whether she finally got where she wanted to go, or just got the joy riding out of her system, will never be known. What is certain is that the man was more than relieved to get his truck back to himself, and never parked inside the cemetery gates again.

The Vanishing Nun

Most vanishing hitchhikers are known to be repeat offenders. They thumb rides time and time again, always traveling the same route or attempting to get to the same destination. One notable exception is the following story, which took place in Chicago during World War II.

It was December 1941. A cab driver was cruising the downtown area one evening, perhaps hoping to find a fare among the remaining Christmas shoppers. Instead, he was hailed by a nun who stood alone on the curb, still and dark against the swirling white snowflakes and colorful Christmas lights.

The nun got into the cab and told the driver where she wished to go. The address was a rather isolated location in the extreme southwest of the city. The driver acknowledged the request and pulled back into traffic.

As the two rode along together, they listened to the radio and discussed the recent and shocking news about the invasion of Pearl Harbor. The cab wound its way through suburban streets that were increasingly dark and quiet. Finally, on a virtually deserted road, the nun directed the driver to turn. He was surprised: he hadn't even noticed the turnoff, which was almost completely obscured by foliage. "This is the driveway," she explained, as they passed through the brush and discovered a long, paved path that led through the trees to a massive stone building. The cab driver then turned to say something in response, and was greeted with the shock of his life. The back seat was empty. The nun had vanished.

Not knowing what else to do, the trembling man drove up to the front of the building, which he soon discovered to be a convent. He went to the door to ask about his fare, and was so obviously distraught that the nuns immediately ushered him inside.

Within the convent, there was a wall devoted to beautifully framed portraits of several nuns. As the cab driver related his strange tale to the Mother Superior, his gaze happened upon the pictures. Immediately, he recognized one of the kind faces.

"That's her!" he exclaimed. "That's the nun who was in my cab tonight!"

The Mother Superior turned to the photo at which the cab driver was pointing. Her careful composure slipped somewhat as she replied, "That can't be." She then explained gently to the man that the nun who had been in his cab had been dead for 10 years.

The sister's spirit had wanted to go home and, apparently, found peace in doing so. For, with the exception of that strange December night, there have been no reports of that nun ever again needing a ride.

Beware of strangers seeking rides on deserted streets. You can never be sure that they're not dangerous—or dead.

The Evergreen Teen

Somewhere in the Evergreen Cemetery, in Evergreen Park, is the grave of a girl who refuses to let death rob her of her adventurous spirit. For nearly 20 years now, she has been venturing beyond the cemetery gates and searching for excitement in downtown Chicago.

Numerous drivers have reported encountering the dark-haired, teenaged hitchhiker. She's been picked up at a number of different locations in the suburbs—but one thing always remains the same. As the drivers near the girl's destination, they are startled and confused to discover that she has disappeared from the vehicle. It is only then that they realize they have been traveling and chatting with a phantom.

The Evergreen Teen might be classified as a typical "vanishing hitchhiker," but she shows a measure of resourcefulness that sets her apart. She doesn't always rely upon the charity of strangers to get where she needs to go. On occasions when she can't thumb a ride, she's been known to actually sneak aboard Chicago Transit Authority buses.

One memorable incident occurred when an eagle-eyed driver noticed he had a passenger who had not paid her fare. The man stopped the bus and marched down the aisle to confront the insolent teen. The girl, no doubt short of cash and seeing no graceful way out of the situation, chose simply to vanish before the eyes of the unbelieving bus driver and all his passengers.

With any luck, she found a less observant bus driver, and was able to continue her day's adventure.

The Flapper

She is nameless, but well-known: the bright, beguiling girl has spent nearly 70 years strolling along Chicago's DesPlaines Avenue in search of a lift. Those who have met her vividly recall her sensational appearance. They tell of a flirty, made-up young woman with stylish, brunette, chin-length tresses. She wears a gaily colored sheath, and shows plenty of shapely leg. Confident and outrageous, she is a throwback to the Roaring Twenties. Known simply as "the Flapper," she has been a resident spirit of the city's South Side since thumbing her first ride in 1933.

By all accounts, the Flapper is forever in search of an evening on the dance floor. Numerous drivers have reported escorting her to the Melody Mill Ballroom, or, after closing time, back home.

Her home is the Jewish Waldheim Cemetery in Forest Park, where she can sometimes be glimpsed by the front gates or entering the mausoleum. She is never there long, though. The thought of a lively party soon lures her away—at which point another unwitting motorist encounters this charming young flapper sashaying down the road, and offers her a ride that he will never forget.

Chapter 3

RIVER WRAITHS

*With its western border carved
by the Mississippi, and its northern
connection to the Great Lakes,
Illinois is a state defined by its
waterways. The rivers and lakes were
tremendous forces in determining
economy, industry and culture—and
provided appropriately dank settings
for many stories of the supernatural.*

*So jump in! The water's fine—just a
little on the haunted side.*

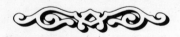

The Eastland Tragedy

For decades it has been said that the Clark Street Bridge in Chicago is a place of disquiet. Walking near the bridge on a still day, one gets the eerie feeling that the surroundings are a thin cover cast over a disturbing underlying reality, and that the fabric of the present might at any moment disintegrate and unveil a terrible past. If conditions are right, and the listener is sensitive, anguished cries may even be heard rising from the water beneath the bridge. They are the echoes of the worst disaster to take place on the Great Lakes in recent time.

In 1915, Western Electric employees planned a summer picnic in Michigan City, Indiana. Five steamboats were chartered to take the revelers across the lake. Early in the morning of July 24, the passengers gathered on the docks on the Chicago River and began to board the vessels.

The *Eastland* was the first to load, and more than 2500 passengers had embarked by the time the gangplank was lifted. Only moments later, disaster struck.

What caused that disaster was a combination of many factors, including the original construction of the ship. The *Eastland* had been built for speed, according to a design which ultimately made her extremely unstable and top-heavy. Later modifications (including, ironically, nearly 14 tons of lifeboats and rafts added to the top deck as a result of new safety regulations following the sinking of the *Titanic*) further increased the ship's high center of gravity. In addition, the *Eastland*'s gangways were so low that the ship would easily take on water if she listed, and the ballast

Raising *S.S. Eastland*
Chicago River

MAX STEIN-CH

Raising the Eastland, *following the disaster in which nearly 850 people lost their lives. (Courtesy of the Eastland Disaster Historical Society.)*

compartments were inadequate and could not quickly respond to changes in weight distribution as passengers moved about. The ship had a history of near accidents, and according to the Eastland Disaster Historical Society was "essentially... a disaster waiting to happen."

On that July morning, when the *Eastland* may have taken on more than her maximum passenger capacity, it finally did happen. The steamer had just left the dock and begun to make its way toward the lake when it suddenly capsized.

Cheers became screams as people spilled off the deck into the Chicago River. Inside the *Eastland*, the situation was even more horrific. Hundreds of passengers were trapped within the over-turned ship and covered almost immediately by tons of water. It was a prison from which very few escaped.

The life-saving efforts were valiant, but before long there was nothing to be done but recover the bodies of those who had drowned. City workers stretched nets across the river to keep the corpses from floating downstream, and divers spent hours working at the gruesome task of retrieving the dead. The bodies were wrapped in sheets and temporarily laid out at the 2nd Regiment Armory, where the agonizing process of identification began. Nearly 850 people died in the Chicago River that day, including many entire families. The *Titanic,* which met her famous end only three years earlier, went down with 1522 souls. Clearly, the sinking of the *Eastland* was a great catastrophe.

Today, those who lost their lives aboard the *Eastland* are recognized with a commemorative plaque. The victims are also remembered in the tales that continue to be told of haunting cries near the Clark Street Bridge.

Over the years, another ghostly rumor about the *Eastland's* dead has emerged. The 2nd Regiment Armory, which served as a temporary morgue on the day of the catastrophe, eventually became the home of Harpo Studios and The Oprah Winfrey Show. Several written accounts have claimed that Winfrey and her employees have experienced strange occurrences and impressions in the building, which have been attributed to encounters with spirits of the ill-fated *Eastland.* But according to one of Winfrey's publicists, Jerilyn Schultz, the reports have no basis in fact.

"These stories come up every year," Schultz said. "But all seems quiet to us."

It may be that there are no specters wandering around Harpo Studios. There is little doubt, however, that the entire city of Chicago bears some psychic mark of the unforgettable sinking of the *Eastland.* For when a celebration turns so quickly to calamity, it takes time for the dead to rest in peace.

A Devilish Spot on the Mississippi

In the earliest days of travel on the Mississippi, boats of all kinds were forced to deal with a narrow and treacherous stretch of river in the southwest corner of Illinois near what is now Grand Tower. Before the river was dammed, flatboat crews found it necessary to leave their craft and walk along the shore, carefully towing their vessel along with sturdy ropes. It was the only way to negotiate the dangerous stretch of murky water.

Fortunately for the boatmen, two distinctive rock formations, colorfully named the "Devil's Backbone" and the "Devil's Bake Oven," marked the perilous route. Unfortunately, the same stony landmarks also served as excellent hiding places for river pirates, who used the rocks as lookout points from which they could see potential victims coming along the Mississippi for miles.

The rocks marked the bottleneck in the river that provided the thieves with a natural ambush spot. As the boat crews slowed and disembarked to avoid the river's hazards, the well-prepared pirates would steal their cargo and leave the passengers and crew either stranded or murdered. Their horrible crimes continued until the mid-1800s, when increased settlement of the area made it impossible for the pirates to operate unnoticed.

The little town of Grand Tower grew steadily. As a busy river port where goods could be shipped and received, it was a natural location for industry. By the late 19th century, iron was big business. The ore was shipped in from Missouri, and the coal to run the furnaces from nearby Murphysboro. At one point, an iron foundry was built atop the Devil's Bake Oven, along with a beautiful two-story home for the superintendent of the business. One century later, all that would remain was a few foundation stones—and a ghost story.

The story is that one of the foundry superintendents had a beautiful, young daughter. Her parents doted on her and, perhaps unwisely, kept her very sheltered from the harsh realities of life. One day, despite their best intentions, the girl fell in love with a most unsuitable suitor—a young man with charm and good looks, but no moral fibre or sense of responsibility. When the superintendent forbade their courtship, the girl simply resorted to sneaking away at night to see her lover. Enraged, the father confined his daughter to the house, and the rogue was convinced to leave town.

The lovelorn young woman languished in the lovely home which had become her prison. From her bedroom window she watched the river and wept, until finally she could go on no longer. The cause may have been disease or pure grief, but the girl died alone, waiting for the return of her lost love.

Sadly, death did not ease her suffering. Not long after the funeral, locals began to see a misty female form on the pathway near the house. In the full light of the moon, she was often identified as the superintendent's daughter. The lonely spirit would always glide along the pathway, and then vanish into the brush. Her appearance would be accompanied by mournful crying on most nights, but when storm clouds filled the sky and lightening pierced the air, the girl's cries became dreadful, bone-chilling screams.

Many years later, the superintendent's house was demolished, but the spirit of the girl continued to haunt the location.

Today, the landscape has changed, and landmarks are no longer needed to guide river boat crews through the devilish spot on the Mississippi. Gone too are the bloodthirsty pirates and their victims. But the ghost of the superintendent's daughter remains, eternally mourning her lost love.

The Spectral Steamboat

In the 1800s, wherever there were waterways, steamboats were a common method of travel and transport. The Spoon River in Fulton County, however, was considered too small to safely accommodate the big boats. There was one time when a group of travelers ignored the common sense rules of the river—and the results were tragic.

Sometime in the 1840s, the Spoon River rose dramatically after a particularly heavy runoff from the nearby hills. A group of ill-advised but adventurous souls viewed the swollen river as a golden opportunity for an excursion. They boarded a light, steam-propelled hunting boat and began down the river.

On April 20, 1889, the *St. Louis Republican* related that many of the locals along the route had never seen a steamboat before in their lives, and were terrified when they heard its "wheezing labors and bantam whistle." Still others were fascinated and drawn to the shore by the jubilant sound of the passengers' singing. The song "Sweet By and By" was, in fact, the last sound heard from the little steamer's deck as it sailed out of sight into the wilderness.

That very night, the water levels fell as quickly as they had risen.

People worried and waited for the return of the boat, but it would have been impossible for the craft to wend its way back: the river had again become a shallow trickle. Rumors spread that the steamer had run aground miles from civilization, and that a terrible fate had befallen its passengers. The grim speculation destroyed all hope for the return of the vessel. The boat was never recovered, and the passengers were never seen again.

Except once.

In the spring of 1853, the Spoon River became swollen with runoff once again. And once again, people living nearby were startled by the distinctive whistle of a steamboat. This time, however, it was heard around midnight. Curious folks gathered along the riverbank, wanting to see who was foolhardy enough to ride the high water into sure disaster. As the boat came into sight, they could hardly believe their eyes.

It was the very steamer that had disappeared years earlier. It moved silently upon the river, and in the darkness appeared "misty white" to the spectators gathered on shore. As the glowing craft came closer to the group, four "visions" appeared on deck. Spotlessly attired in gleaming white, they were radiant and beautiful. They gazed downriver and began sweetly to sing. Those who watched from the shoreline would never forget the lyrics: "In the Sweet By and By."

There were two men on shore who could not accept what they were seeing. Determined to rescue the long-lost boaters, they jumped into a skiff and rowed quickly toward the larger craft. They became increasingly cold as they approached the steamer, and suddenly found themselves enclosed in heavy mist. The music swelled around them, but in the fog they completely lost sight of the boat they were trying to reach. Unable to see their target, and unnerved by the frenzied voices on shore begging them to return, the men rowed back to the bank.

Once ashore, the men were told that they had actually collided with the spectral vessel. The skiff showed no damage, of course, but there was evidence of contact on the men's clothing. It was soaking wet from being enveloped in the heavy, white mist.

Knowing there was nothing it could do, the crowd watched in silence as the phantom steamboat floated down the river and out of sight. It would never be seen again, but it would never be forgotten, either. With so many witnesses, the story spread far and wide. The "Mystery of Spoon River" remains a gem in Fulton County folklore.

The Spoon River in Fulton County remains too small for large crafts. During one heavy spring runoff in the 1840s, a group of adventurers ignored the warnings, and suffered the consequences.

The Sad Spirit of Lizzie Clark

The year was 1876. In Dallas City, an orphaned teen named Lizzie Clark was working at the Riverside Hotel. Her employers were generally believed to be unscrupulous characters involved in dirty business deals and possibly even criminal activity. Lizzie was the proverbial beggar who could not afford to be choosy, and so she slaved away at her daily tasks, saving what money she could to finance her plan of eventual escape. Unfortunately, as time went on, leaving her job appeared more and more risky. The longer she worked at the Riverside, the more she learned about her employers' crimes. And the more she knew, the more she feared that they would never allow her to leave.

Then came the day when Lizzie vanished. She was last seen walking up the stairs of the hotel one afternoon. A search of the building and area turned up no clue to her whereabouts, and those sympathetic to her plight hoped that Lizzie Clark had finally made good her escape. That hope was dashed when it was discovered that Lizzie's hard-earned savings—about $200—were still securely tucked away in her room. People whispered that the hapless girl had met with foul play, and that her body had likely been thrown into the Mississippi and swept away.

Lizzie's spirit, however, would not be so summarily disposed of. Rumors began circulating about how the girl's ghost had been sighted wandering around the islands in the Mississippi, clad in a white, diaphanous gown. In the thin light of early morning or late evening, she could be seen running across the upper deck of an old beached steamboat, her eyes wide with terror, her throat

In the 1800s, steamboats were a common sight on the Mississippi River. Lizzie Clark's suffering spirit was seen on the deck of one similar to this.

bruised and bloody. Witnesses heard her screaming, "Leave me alone, leave me alone, or I will drown myself!" The ethereal shape would then throw herself from the deck of the steamer into the waters below.

For years, the tale of Lizzie Clark's unavenged murder and anguished return was a staple for storytellers in Hancock County. Then, in 1915, the narrative that had been repeated for nearly four decades received an unexpected update.

At the foot of Oak Street, in Dallas City, a parcel of land was being prepared as a boat landing. As the grader worked to level the lot, a gruesome discovery was made: it was a shallow, stony grave, containing the skeletal remains of a woman and some shreds of green cloth. A number of old-timers in the area came forward to report that Lizzie Clark had worn a coat made of bright green material, and it was decided that the remains were quite likely hers. No doubt in response to morbid interest in the case, the bones and cloth were on public display for some time after the discovery.

The discovery created as many questions as it answered. Lizzie Clark had definitely been murdered. People still suspected her employers of the terrible deed. But what about the scene reenacted time after time on the deck of the beached steamboat? If Lizzie truly did throw herself into the Mississippi, did the wicked hoteliers go to the trouble of fishing her out, only to dispose of her body in a shallow pit?

Perhaps it will take a reappearance of the ghost herself to answer these questions.

The Shrieking Wraith

The two men had heard all the stories, and, feeling brave while in the safety of familiar surroundings and the company of others, had decided to investigate the matter for themselves. Now they sat among the ruins of the old mill, watching and waiting, on an eerie moonlit night. They shivered in the cold. Midnight approached.

Suddenly an anguished voice cut through the frosty air. "Don't, Jack! You can have the money! Don't—" The terrified screams became a strangled gurgling, followed by silence. It was a brief silence, broken when the hideous apparition of a man clothed in rags sprang up before the two horror-stricken witnesses. His face was chalky and his eyes were "set and stony." The wraith shrieked in agony and clawed helplessly with skeletal fingers at the gushing wound on its neck. Then, with one final look at the two petrified men, the shade screamed once more, turned and vanished into the old mill. According to the *St. Louis Republican* (April 20, 1889), the ghost hunters rushed back to the security of Lewistown, "not caring to make further investigation."

The men had just been with the ghost of Duncan's Mill, a phantom quite famous for many years in that area. The legend went that, long ago, two fishermen who had been casting nets near the ruins of the mill began arguing over money. The fight became physical and, according to the St. Louis Republican, one man used a boat hook to "beat the other's head into a jelly." He then slit the man's throat and fled, leaving the battered, blood-drenched body of his fishing companion dead in the boat. The murderer was never captured and the victim was never identified. His body was buried near the site of his demise.

Soon afterward, people who lived near the abandoned mill began to report hearing wretched cries in the night and seeing a mysterious, shrouded figure. It was said that on any calm night around harvest time, the miserable spirit of the murdered man could be heard and perhaps even seen. But, as the two adventurers from Lewistown could attest, it was an experience that any sane person would wish to avoid.

The Boatman

One year early in the 1860s, the Mississippi River was on what the old-timers referred to as "a tear." Every day, it challenged its banks further as an uncontrollable amount of spring runoff flooded into it. The water crept higher and higher, until residents along the shore found themselves abandoning their wagons for boats. Some evacuated, but those of a more stubborn nature simply took refuge on the second floors of their houses. Anywhere people wanted to go, they traveled by boat.

South of Warsaw, the low-lying pastures were completely submerged. A group of ranchers became concerned about stock they kept on the Missouri side of the river near Alexandria. At the height of the flood, they rented a boat and rowed across the swollen river in an attempt to save as many animals as possible from drowning.

All afternoon they worked at leading the stock to higher ground. By the time they had finished, night had fallen and a bright moon cast its reflection over the expanse of water. As the men prepared to journey back, they noticed that they were quite alone. There was not another boat to be seen or heard.

As they rowed along in the silence, one of the men suddenly shouted out, "My God, boys, look ahead of you there!" Every man in the group turned to look, and later every one would swear to having seen the same thing.

It was a strange, old-fashioned craft. It passed soundlessly not more than 20 feet in front of them. The boat had a shadowy, filmy appearance and seemed to be covered in moss and weeds. But it was the boatman himself who made the ranchers' blood run cold. Neither the misty quality of his flowing beard, nor the way he worked the translucent oars in a nearly robotical fashion terrified them most; most terrifying of all was his face, grim and staring. The men would later say that he had the face of a corpse.

As the spectral boat glided by, the men could see it held a large bundle, covered in a luminous white sheet. The ranchers pointed and gasped, but the eerie boatman made no acknowledgment of the group. Two of the bravest fellows called out to him, but the old man only stared fixedly ahead and continued to ply the oars.

This was too much for one of the ranchers to bear. Swearing that he was going to see what it was, he pulled out a revolver and fired six rapid shots at the figure. All made their mark. None did any damage, but the action did manage to capture the boatman's attention.

The gruesome specter threw down his oars, and turned to fix his cold, dead stare on the group of men. His wizened features contorted as he let loose a ghastly, mocking laugh. Then, abruptly, the dreadful phantom and his craft vanished.

The terrified ranchers finished their journey as quickly as they could. They arrived pale, shaking, and anxious to unburden themselves of their strange tale. After sharing the frightening account, the men half expected to be ridiculed. Instead, they were met with wide-eyed belief, and an explanation of who the ghost was.

The story was that there once lived a fisherman in a lonely cabin over on the Missouri shore. He saw few people other than the daughter he lived with, and that girl was the sole light of the old man's life. Sadly, one spring, the girl died of a strange disease, and her father was so stricken with grief that he lost his senses. It was said that he carefully wrapped the body in a shroud, placed it in the bottom of his fishing boat, and rowed away down the Mississippi, never to be seen again—never to be seen alive, that is.

There are no reports of the phantom boatman ever appearing again, but the story told by the ranchers was retold for decades. Perhaps some spring, when the Mississippi is pushing at her banks, someone will meet him again.

Chapter 4

GHOSTLY REVENGE

Hollywood's favorite type of spirit is one with a mission, and what better mission is there than revenge?

Though they are not driven by the ever-elusive movie deal, many ghosts do seem to stay on this earth for the purpose of punishing those who have done them wrong. It may be one reason why the act of murder so often results in a haunting.

Revenge, it is said, is a dish best served cold—and there is nothing colder than a phantom touch.

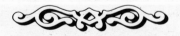

Spirits from the Slaughter

You may be an undigested bit of beef.... There's more
of gravy than of grave about you, whatever you are!
—Charles Dickens, *A Christmas Carol*

When Ebenezer Scrooge uttered these delightfully unforgettable lines, he was blaming ordinary indigestion for the
apparition haunting him at that moment. But here's another
thought: could a "bit of beef," digested or not, come back to
haunt you in its own right? Most people think of meat as tidily
cut portions neatly encased in plastic wrap, which originate in
the grocer's cooler. But the animals from which those portions
come were once alive. If animals have a spiritual essence—and
many believe that they do—could they not return as ghosts,
unhappy about their fate?

At least three examples from Chicago suggest they can.

Thurston's, a bar on West George Street, was once a slaughterhouse. The nightspot was plagued by the spirits of butchered
animals until recently, after a priest was asked to bless the premises.

In the 1950s, a butcher named Jesse Roe quit his job in a
Chicago slaughterhouse because of a spectral sheep that would
charge at him across the parking lot and then vanish into thin air.
"Do dumb animals have spirits and souls?" he was quoted as asking. "Can they come back from the dead to haunt you?" At least
one of Roe's fellow workers believed so; a man named Frank also
chose to give up his paycheck rather than risk further encounters
with the vengeful ewe.

But it was another Chicago butcher, Gordon Yates, who related the most disconcerting of the three stories. In the spring of 1953, he worked in a butcher shop that had a haunted walk-in refrigerator.

Yates had been employed by the shop for only a few weeks when he first experienced the unusual phenomenon. He had just butchered and trimmed a side of beef and carried it into the refrigerator, where it was hung on a hook. He walked out, closed the door, and returned to the cutting block. And that was when he first heard the strange, low sounds emanating from the large cooler. He stopped working and listened carefully, and what he heard made his blood run cold. Yates knew the various stages of meat production: the sounds were unmistakably the cries of cows fearfully awaiting slaughter. He pulled open the refrigerator door, half-expecting to see a fellow employee playing a prank, and the noise immediately stopped. When the door was closed once more, the eerie lowing continued.

Yates was understandably mystified and called several fellow employees over to listen with him. Once the group assembled, the refrigerator stood silent, leaving Yates feeling foolish and all the more perplexed. When the other butchers returned to their work, one lingered long enough to offer Gordon Yates a warning. "I wouldn't work on this station for double my salary," he was quoted as saying. "Funny things have been going on here for years."

When Yates pressed the man for details, he learned that the last meat cutter to work the station had left because he claimed that the walk-in refrigerator was haunted.

"Haunted!" Even after what he had just experienced, Gordon Yates was incredulous. The other man was insistent.

"A few years ago a butcher who worked this block was found dead in that box. It turned out that the door closed after him and somehow he was trapped. No one noticed he hadn't punched out

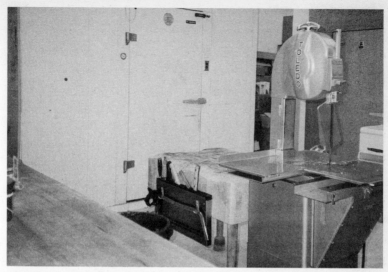

In 1953, Gordon Yates worked in a butcher shop with a walk-in meat locker, like this one. The main difference was that Yates's locker was haunted.

when everyone knocked off work for the day. The next morning they found him. Sometimes, that inside door handle doesn't work. If I were you, I'd be careful of it."

The eerie tale replayed itself in Gordon Yates's mind until quitting time, but, thankfully, he heard no more mournful animal sounds from the cooler.

Early the following morning, Yates was about to carry a side of beef into the refrigerator when the phenomenon began again. The distinct sounds of mooing cattle began to seep from within the cooler. Desperate to make them stop, Yates yanked open the heavy door. This time, the sounds did not cease. They grew louder as the nervous man walked into the refrigerator to hang the beef. He was surrounded by the baleful animal cries, entangled in them. Then he turned around and realized that he truly was about to be trapped.

The massive insulated door of the refrigerator had begun to swing shut. Gordon Yates remembered his co-worker's warning about how the inside handle didn't always work, and made a desperate lunge for it. He managed to grab the lever just before it fell, and pushed at the door, but it seemed to resist him. Yates had to brace his entire weight against the door, which had always swung freely before; still he managed to open it just enough to squeeze out of the cooler. Once out, Gordon Yates realized that he could never walk back into that refrigerator again. He removed his apron and promptly resigned.

If Yates questioned the sanity of his decision, he did not do so for long. Only a few days later, he learned that the butcher who had taken his job was found dead in the haunted refrigerator. Investigators tested the inside handle and found it in good working order, so the death remained a mystery.

One year later, the walk-in cooler claimed a third victim. Faced with the potential walk-out of their entire staff, the owners of the butcher shop finally had the unit rebuilt, and the door replaced, although no mechanical problem was ever found. The death toll ended there, but the stories remained and no employee ever wanted to work at that particular station again.

Mrs. Gray's Curse

In the mid-19th century, the city of Peoria was only a village. Most of its inhabitants were challenged by a hard life of surviving the elements and working the land. On one particular day in 1847, an old woman named Mrs. Gray felt herself completely beaten by this difficult existence. Her vegetable gardens had been destroyed by scavengers, year after year. Each cold winter worsened the crippling ache in the old woman's joints. Her lazy nephew lived under her roof without ever contributing a dime, and a young local lawyer who had handled some of the boy's legal problems had just foreclosed on the Gray's prized home, in lieu of a payment that could not be made. The elderly couple packed their few belongings and prepared to go, but Mrs. Gray was intent upon leaving something behind. She hobbled purposefully into her backyard, raised her fists defiantly in the air and uttered a bitter curse: "May this land turn into thorns and thistles, and bring ill luck, sickness and death to its every owner!" Her rage somewhat vented, Mrs. Gray climbed aboard the creaky wagon. She and her husband then left Peoria forever, but for 77 more years, her hex would blight the land.

The lawyer, who never lived on the property and moved to Bloomington shortly after acquiring it, escaped the old lady's wrath. Countless others who tried to make a home there were not so lucky. Time and time again, disaster struck, just as the crone predicted.

The first family to rent the old Gray place was ex-Governor Thomas Ford and his wife. They lived there peacefully enough for a few years, but in 1865 endured a double tragedy. Both their sons were murdered—the elder boy, for reasons unknown, and the younger, while searching for his big brother's killer. Soon after, Mr. and Mrs. Ford were said to have died of grief.

For many years, the house sat empty and neglected, overgrown by weeds and overrun by rats. Finally, one winter night, during a blizzard, the building inexplicably burned to the ground. Amidst the driving snow and fiery timbers, some claimed to see an old woman frolicking merrily in the flames.

Shortly after the Civil War, the property was repurchased for back-taxes and became home to a freedman named Tom Lindsey. Lindsey moved a sturdy old shack onto the foundation of the former house, and settled in happily. Within months, however, the little shanty was struck by lightening and destroyed. Lindsey rebuilt, but this time protected himself with a petrified rabbit's foot and a pile of horseshoes. With his good-luck charms spread about the house, the man managed to enjoy 25 tranquil years there.

The banker who bought the property after Tom Lindsey's death was not so well armed or so fortunate. The man built a grand house, one suitable, he felt, for someone of his standing. He then married a lovely young woman and had a child. All seemed perfect, but just a few months later, the curse struck. The banker's wife and child both died, of some unknown disease. A year after that, the man remarried, and his second wife quickly became pregnant. But when the baby was born, it cried endlessly, and soon died as well. The young mother was so distraught that she had to be permanently hospitalized.

The bereaved banker moved away, leaving the door open for more doomed tenants. The place was turned into a boarding house where, once again, misery was prevalent. The woman who operated the business lost two children during her stay. Her daughter drowned in a nearby lake, and her young son died of his injuries after falling from a balcony. The house was then rented to some milliners who complained that the house had an offensive odor. They tried to track down the source of the smell, but were never successful. They moved out after a short time, escaping relatively unscathed.

In 1894, the cursed land got another new owner: the Peoria Public Library. A brand new building was constructed the following year, but it didn't break the string of bad luck. The first librarian, E. S. Willcox, was struck and killed by a streetcar. The man who followed him, S. Patterson Prouse, died of a heart attack during a board meeting. Prouse's successor, Dr. Edwin Wiley, had the job for only three years before accidentally ingesting some poison in 1924.

Dr. Wiley was the last of Peoria's librarians reported to have died an untimely death, so perhaps Mrs. Gray finally became content with the body count. But some believe that the old woman still remains on what was once her plot of land. The director of a library in another county recalled his days working in Peoria:

Entire shelves of books would be upset, for no reason. And there were other things. Once I had a pile of papers sitting on the desk, in my office. I was just standing there—and there was no breeze, no open window—and these papers just flew up in the air and landed on the floor.

Papers can be picked up, and books can be re-shelved. Current employees of the Peoria Public Library might count themselves lucky that Mrs. Gray is restricting herself to such minor mischief these days.

Justice for Louisa

The Chicago Homicide Record Index has an entry for the date of May 1, 1897. The name of the deceased is shown to be Mrs. Louisa Luetgert. Under the heading "other persons involved," the name Adolph Luetgert appears. Adolph was Louisa's husband, and following a dramatic trial, he was found guilty of her murder.

The Luetgerts were a wealthy couple who lived in a splendid mansion on the corner of Hermitage and Diversey. Their money came from sausage—at that time, Adolph Luetgert owned and operated the largest sausage factory in the city. But despite the fancy home and lucrative business, the Luetgert's relationship was not harmonious. When Louisa vanished on that first day of May, Adolph was immediately under suspicion. And when the poor woman's wedding ring and some human remains were discovered in a potash vat in the basement of her husband's factory, the arrest was made.

The prosecutors accused Adolph of boiling his wife's body in the vat and cremating her bones in the factory's huge furnace. That act was gruesome enough, but the rumors that people spread throughout the city were worse. The real truth, storytellers whispered, was that Adolph had ground Louisa into sausage. It was a tale with no basis in fact, but was so widely believed that sausage sales suffered dramatically for at least six months after the trial.

When Adolph Luetgert was found guilty of the murder, he was packed off to Joliet State Penitentiary with a life sentence. It seemed that justice had been served—but at least one person felt that Adolph deserved to be punished further. When the new inmate arrived at his prison cell, he found the ghost of his wife waiting to haunt him.

Adolph Luetgert expected prison life to be hard, but he never counted on being tormented every single moment. When the man tried to read or think, his concentration would be broken by Louisa's ominous, ghostly whispers. When he tried to close his eyes and sleep, he would feel the icy breeze that indicated her presence, or the smooth, terrifying touch of cold, dead fingers on his flesh. Upon opening his eyes in the dark, he would be shocked by the frightening, filmy, white apparition of his dead wife, her lips pressed into a cruel sneer, her eyes glowing with contempt. Adolph complained repeatedly to prison officials, but was casually dismissed. Eventually, when Louisa's torments became more than he could bear, Adolph escaped by the only means available to him: death. Adolph Luetgert's life sentence had turned out to be only two years long.

Louisa Luetgert had had her revenge but, surprisingly, did not find eternal rest. After Adolph's death, the woman's spirit moved to more familiar surroundings—the mansion where she had once lived. Her misty, white form was often seen standing peacefully by the mantelpiece in the living room. Louisa no longer engaged in the threatening behavior she had shown her murderous husband, but the new owner of the mansion was displeased, nonetheless. To rid his home of the pesky spirit, he had the building moved to a new address on Marshfield Avenue. For a time, the extreme and unusual tactic worked—Louisa stopped dropping by Luetgert Mansion. That did not mean, however, that she had stopped making spectral appearances.

Louisa's next haunt was the sausage factory where her murder had very likely taken place. On several occasions, night watchmen at the factory encountered the woman's white apparition drifting through the area in the basement near the potash vat and furnace where her remains had been found. She seemed to mean no harm, and perhaps she did no harm—but the factory that had made the

Luetgerts wealthy was destroyed in a fire in 1902. The cause of the fire would always be a complete mystery.

With the sausage factory reduced to smoking rubble, Louisa Luetgert was once again a spirit without a home. She returned to her former residence (despite its new location), and she was as unwelcome as before. Again the owner tried to evade Louisa by literally "moving house." This time, the mansion was transported back nearly to its original location. Either this pleased Louisa Luetgert, or her spirit simply felt no further need to roam, for her fireside appearances virtually stopped.

Since then, the ghost is still reported to make one annual visit to her home. Those who wish to encounter the late Louisa Luetgert might be able to do so each year on the first of May, the anniversary of her disappearance. No doubt, she returns to remind people of her untimely demise. After all, Louisa was not a woman to let an important matter drop.

The Vengeful Ghosts of Canton

Greenwood Cemetery in Canton, Illinois, is home to a strange and sad ghost story that is more than a century old. It began with a tragic accident, reported in the *Canton Daily Register* on June 29, 1899.

CRUSHED TO DEATH—Little Son of Thomas Chell, the Sexton, Killed at Greenwood Cemetery—IRON GATE FELL ON HIM—Skull Was Crushed, Internal Injuries Sustained, and Consciousness Was Not Recovered—Death Ensued Quickly—Gate Was Leaning Against Stone Pillar, with Hinges Broken—Had Been in That Condition Since Wednesday Night.

This stone marks the grave of little Eddie Chell, who, according to local lore, was killed by ghosts seeking revenge against his father.

The article went on in great detail about the terrible event, explaining that Sexton Chell had taken his eight-year-old boy, Edward, to work with him that morning. Father and son examined the broken gate, and the elder Chell walked to a nearby tool shed to find something that would secure it. Suddenly, there was a terrific crash. Thomas Chell spun around, and was greeted by the most horrifying sight of his life. The massive iron gate had toppled over, and crushed beneath it was little Eddie.

Thomas Chell managed to lift the gate and pull his son from beneath it. He rushed the unconscious youngster to the nearest home, and five of the city's doctors were summoned immediately. They worked on the boy for more than an hour—their procedures, and the child's injuries, were described in painful detail by the *Daily Register*—but were unable to save his life. Young William Edward Chell, age eight, was buried near the mausoleum in the cemetery where his father worked.

The coroner decided that, since there were no witnesses, it would be necessary to hold an inquest. That very afternoon, the evidence was examined and a verdict delivered. It was concluded that the death had been accidental. Throughout the inquest, the grief-stricken Thomas Chell maintained that he could not understand how the accident had happened: the heavy gate had been leaning back against its stone pillar, and Edward had not touched it. Finally, at a loss for any other explanation, he weakly suggested that a gust of wind might have caused the gate to fall. This suggestion made little sense, however, given that the ornate gate weighed 500 pounds.

Nearly one month later, another article in the *Canton Daily Register* led the people of the city to a different conclusion. On July 22, 1899, Greenwood Cemetery was once again in the news, this time for a political gaffe regarding an ill-planned restructuring of the cemetery. The article began with the following sentence:

Greenwood Cemetery today.

Alderman E.A. Eggleston, chairman of the public buildings and grounds committee of the city council, frankly admits that it was a mistake to remove the bodies buried on the old free lots in Greenwood Cemetery without giving public notice and allowing ample time for friends and relatives to act in the matter.

The city had been digging up bodies in the free lots, and depositing them in trenches in a less desirable portion of the cemetery. The vacated plots on prime land were then being resold at high prices, although Alderman Eggleston sincerely assured the public that profit "was not especially considered" when the reorganization was planned. Certainly, it was not the only consideration, for months earlier the alderman had reserved one of the prime plots for himself.

The uproar in council chambers might have attracted little attention, had Edward Chell's recent death not been lingering in the minds of Canton's citizens. People with superstitious imaginations began to speculate that, as sexton of the cemetery, Thomas Chell must have had a great deal to do with the exhumation of those graves. Were the souls that had been resting peacefully there angered? Did they take their revenge on Sexton Chell by murdering his son? Was that a possible explanation for the accident which, so far, had none?

According to one Canton historian, people answered these questions in the affirmative, and adopted the story of Greenwood's vengeful ghosts into their folklore. In the end, people never could accept that little Eddie Chell had died for no reason and with no apparent explanation.

The real explanation will never be known, because today Greenwood Cemetery is a restful and quiet place that promises to never give up its secrets.

The Unstoppable Charles Vaughn

Mrs. Sally Vaughn of Chicago was an unhappy woman. Her marriage to her husband Charles had become a joyless routine in which she did all the work and he had all the pleasure. In particular, she had grown weary of the robust construction worker's endless sexual appetite. After 10 children and many years of performing what she considered to be her "marital duty," Sally decided to end it. In 1943, she divorced Charles and happily moved on to the next phase of her life.

Charles Vaughn, however, was not so eager to change the status quo. Although the divorce papers had been signed and his ex-wife had a different home, Charles still saw it as his right to drop in, from time to time, and demand a few carnal favors "for old time's sake." If Sally dared to be uncooperative, Charles would become threatening. Thus, despite the divorce, little changed for the next 10 years.

By the summer of 1953, Sally Vaughn was desperate to be rid of her ex-husband. Divorce had accomplished nothing; Sally knew that a more permanent solution was necessary. The opportunity arose when her younger cousin—a soldier on leave from his outfit at Fort Benning, Georgia—came to visit.

The soldier was trained to kill, and this fact repeated itself over and over in Sally Vaughn's mind as the two sat in the sunny kitchen sharing coffee and news. Seeing her only chance to be rid of Charles, she summoned the courage to ask her young relative the shocking question.

"Would you kill my ex-husband for me? I'd give a month's pay for it."

The cousin either knew of Charles Vaughn's despicable behavior, badly needed the money, or had been trained beyond the ability to value human life, for he readily agreed. In fact, he gave Sally a bargain. A month's pay—$90—was excessive, he told her. $50 would do just fine.

That evening, Charles Vaughn was discovered in his apartment, lying in a dark pool of blood. He had been bludgeoned to death with a hammer. It was Tuesday, August 4, 1953.

On the morning of Wednesday, August 5, Sally Vaughn awoke feeling lighter and freer than she had in years. For the first time in her adult life, she had some control over her world. It was exhilarating to know that Charles would not bother her, ever again.

Sally wrapped herself in a robe and strolled into the kitchen to make some toast and coffee. After starting the percolator and getting the bread out of the cupboard, she opened the refrigerator and rummaged around for a jar of her favorite preserves. When she stood up and closed the fridge door, Sally Vaughn was met with the most shocking sight of her life. She shrieked and dropped the jar. Sticky, red fruit compote spread across the clean, white tile.

There stood Charles Vaughn. His hair was matted with blood and his face was bruised and swollen. The man looked more threatening than ever, and quite capable of doing his ex-wife harm. The corpse said nothing, but began to advance on Sally. When he raised his huge hands toward her throat, she found the will to move. Screaming, she ran from the hideous apparition and locked herself securely in the bedroom.

After a considerable amount of time, Sally found the courage to go back to the kitchen. Her ex-husband's ghost was nowhere to be seen but, understandably, the woman was still hysterical. Sally Vaughn had not escaped the abusive Charles through divorce, and now it seemed that she had not escaped him through death. With nowhere left to turn, Sally picked up the telephone and dialed the police.

The detectives who interviewed Sally Vaughn had no interest in her wild ghost story, but were quite curious about her knowledge of the details of Charles Vaughn's murder. They began to question her, and it was not long before the truth spilled out. Sally admitted to everything, and exposed her cousin as well. Indeed, she would have done anything at that point to placate the ghost.

The arrests were made, and Sally Vaughn and her helpful cousin went to prison. Whether the late Charles Vaughn ever felt the need to visit his wife there is, unfortunately, not known.

Chapter 5

ETERNALLY RESTLESS

*Many cemeteries today are beautiful,
landscaped parks. Historical graveyards comfort
us with a sense of permanency, and even small,
run-down burial grounds can be inviting
places of peace. So why do we tend to be so
apprehensive about such lovely locations?*

*Because they're full of the dead.
And sometimes the dead come back.*

*It makes sense that ghosts most often return
to the significant sites of their lives, but there are
many stories suggesting that some spirits are more
attached to their physical remains than their
former homes and possessions.*

*So, remember to whistle when you walk
past the churchyard—and remember these tales
of the eternally restless spirits of Illinois.*

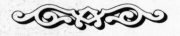

Bachelor's Grove

Southwest of Chicago, at the end of a bare dirt path that can be found about a quarter-mile from the Midlothian Turnpike, is an abandoned cemetery by the name of Bachelor's Grove. This small, nearly inaccessible graveyard hasn't seen a burial for decades. It is far from being forgotten, however, for Bachelor's Grove holds the dubious distinction of being one of the most haunted cemeteries in the world.

Bachelor's Grove was founded in the 1830s, and reportedly named for the scores of single men who broke the nearby land for farming. Situated in the Rubio Woods Forest Preserve, the cemetery is surrounded by a dense thicket of trees and a quarry pond. Originally, it was considered to be a peaceful and private oasis in the forest. Today, "private" feels more like dangerously isolated, and what was once peaceful has become disturbed. Furthermore, no one would now use the term "oasis" to describe this sad, desecrated place. Bachelor's Grove has been terribly damaged over the years, and the damage seems to have resulted in a wild variety of ghostly phenomena. Since the 1950s, more than 100 supernatural incidents have been reported to have happened on this one-acre plot of land. They range from random cold spots and sudden feelings of dread to far more dramatic occurrences.

Bachelor's Grove has been visited and studied by countless psychics, ghost hunters and students of the paranormal, but there is still no consensus on what opened the cemetery's spiritual gates. Many say that the ghostly activity was inevitable, claiming that Bachelor's Grove was built upon ground sacred to Native Americans. Others say that the cemetery's general decline began in the 1920s, when the pond was a rumored dumping ground for gangsters who needed a secluded spot in which to dispose of their victims' bodies. What is a matter of record, rather than rumor, is that vandalism has become a common occurrence since the 1960s. By the 70s, evidence of satanic rituals was routinely found in the cemetery. In the years since, tombstones have been rearranged, thrown into the pond, or stolen. Signs of damage and disrespect are common. Not surprisingly, some families have thought it necessary to move the bodies of their dearly departed to other cemeteries. Today, there are none who go to Bachelor's Grove to visit the grave of a loved one—but there are many who come looking for the ghosts. And the ghosts tend not to disappoint.

Even the most steadfast skeptics will admit that, in this terrible place, it is impossible to shake the feeling that one is being watched. Even more unsettling is the sensation of being touched by invisible, cold hands. But this general sense of having "company," unnerving though it may be, is usually only the tantalizing appetizer in the ghostly repast that the Grove prepares for its guests. Astonishing apparitions are the hearty main course.

One of the most famous phantoms of Bachelor's Grove is known as the "White Lady" or "the Madonna." Some locals have also dubbed her, for no apparent reason, "Mrs. Rogers." When the moon is full, this misty vision is often seen drifting through the woods near the cemetery in a flowing, ivory white gown, with an infant who appears to wail soundlessly in her arms. She is believed to be buried in the Grove, in a grave next to that of her son, by whom she was predeceased.

Other oft-seen specters include a farmer and his plow horse, both of whom drowned in the quarry pond in the late 1800s, a number of quiet figures obscured by dark hooded robes, and a grotesque two-headed man, who some say was hidden away by his family during his time on earth. There are numerous ghost lights that dance among the tombstones, sudden flurries of attacking bats, and a variety of other frightening phenomena. For pure intrigue, however, it's tough to top the phantom house.

For the last half century, many people visiting Bachelor's Grove have encountered what has come to be known as the "vanishing house." It appears in broad daylight, and looks quite solid and real. When people try to approach it, however, it shrinks into the distance, and eventually disappears from sight. Mysteriously, there are no records of a house ever having been built there, and no physical evidence of a foundation of any kind.

Testament to the building's realistic appearance is the fact that many witnesses saw the house without trying to approach it, and were completely unaware of having witnessed anything paranormal. Imagine the shock such people would experience when later hearing or reading about the spectral abode.

Over a period of many decades, numerous people who have seen the house offer nearly identical descriptions of it. One researcher gathered a dozen drawings of the dwelling from unrelated witnesses. They all depicted the same thing—a white, two-story, Victorian-style farmhouse with a porch swing. The house is always surrounded by a picket fence, and there is always a low light that can be seen bleeding through the closed draperies. If only it were possible to get close enough to peek through those windows.

Another common phenomenon associated with Bachelor's Grove occurs not in the cemetery itself, but on the roads nearby. Phantom cars—big, black, 1930s-era sedans—have been encountered near the Midlothian Turnpike. Drivers have often been left shaken and incredulous when such a vehicle approaches and then vanishes before their eyes. Other motorists have had experiences even more frightening, when they've collided with these cars. Several people have reported being sideswiped by a speeding sedan that appeared out of nowhere. They would feel the impact, hear the sound of crumpling metal and breaking glass, and pull over, but upon inspecting their car, they would discover that their automobile had sustained no damage at all. The theory is that these vintage vehicles once belonged to the Chicago gangsters who used the cemetery's quarry pond to hide the grisly evidence of their murderous crimes.

Bachelor's Grove, with its extraordinary variety of anomalous activity, has long been a dream destination for fans and students of the paranormal. The chances of encountering something strange are high, as are the chances of capturing it on film. Many claim to have had great success with spirit photography at the cemetery, offering an assortment of curious images as proof. Some are reported to show ectoplasmic forms rising from the tombstones, or strange, swirling bodies of mist. In other photos, people claim to see faces superimposed on the grave markers. Likely the most famous ghost photo from Bachelor's Grove was taken by Dale Kaczmarek, president of Chicago's well-known Ghost Research Society. Taken with infrared film, it shows the well-defined image of a woman in a flowing white dress, seated on the remains of a tombstone. Some have dismissed the picture as a double exposure, but Kaczmarek, who acknowledges that 90% of photos thought to show a ghost can be explained in some logical way, defends it.

Whether or not anyone has the pictures to prove it, there is little doubt that Bachelor's Grove is haunted. In fact, it is only haunted: not much exists there now except the ghosts. Few headstones remain intact. Each year, the wild plants encroach a little farther on the grounds. Someday, the dirt path will be irretrievably swallowed up by the forest, and then Bachelor's Grove will be forgotten, left to die its own death in the remote silence of the woods.

The Silent Cortege

It was Friday, July 4, 1889. The heat had been oppressive all day, and the evening brought no relief. A woman named Mrs. Chris had a neighbor keeping her company, and the two friends, hoping for even the occasional cooling breeze, decided to sit on the front porch while they talked.

The hour grew late, and a full moon illuminated everything for miles around. Just past 11 pm, the neighbor stopped rocking in her chair, and peered into the distance. "What's that on the road?" she asked.

Mrs. Chris stood up and walked to the weathered porch railing to get a better look. "Wagons," she replied, "from the old fort."

She spoke with a certain amount of disbelief, for Fort de Chartres, near the Chris home, was little more than a ruin. No one ever had business there, let alone at such a late hour.

As the procession grew closer, the silhouettes became clearer and clearer in the bright moonlight. The women counted 40 wagons in total, followed by 13 pairs of horsemen and a number of people soberly trailing behind the cavalcade on foot. Near the front of the procession was a single, low dray. It carried what appeared in the light of the moon to be a casket. A little farther down the road, there was indeed a small cemetery: Mrs. Chris and her neighbor realized at once that they were witnessing a funeral procession.

How strange, for a funeral to be taking place in the middle of the night! The women could not recall hearing of a death in the area, and it still made no sense that the cortege seemed to be coming from the crumbling fort. Furthermore, although the night was bright, it was odd that not one person in the procession carried a lamp. Mrs. Chris and her friend puzzled over the

Today, historic Fort de Chartres has been reconstructed, but in 1889, when two women witnessed a phantom funeral procession coming from it, it was a crumbling ruin.

peculiar situation in hushed tones. When they stopped speaking for a few moments, the greatest mystery of all became apparent.

The funeral cortege was entirely silent.

The women watched in astonishment as wagon wheels ground and bumped along the rough dirt road and horses' hooves raised clouds of dust in the hot air. Not a sound could be heard. People in the procession appeared to speak to one another, but there were no voices. The night was all but still: its silence was broken only by the yelping of the family dog, which became increasingly agitated as it watched the eerie parade.

The next morning, the women discovered that they had not been alone in witnessing the ghostly spectacle. The dog's barking had awakened the neighbor's father, and he had risen to see what the fuss was. From his bedroom window, he too had watched the inexplicable procession, and was able to verify everything the women had seen.

At the restored Fort de Chartres, interpretive scenes like this are common. In 1889, however, historical events were replayed only by the ghosts.

And so, Mrs. Chris and her friend were convinced that they had not been hallucinating. Still, they had no idea what it was they had seen, until several days later, when a visitor who was well versed in the history of Fort de Chartres heard their strange story.

The visiting woman told them of something that had happened roughly 100 years earlier, when the fort was still occupied by the French. A prominent local merchant was killed in a fight with one of the officers of the garrison, and fort officials were unsure how they should handle such a scandalous and potentially volatile situation. They sought advice from the regional government, and received it: the victim was to be buried quietly, at midnight, in a local cemetery. Only the light of the moon would be used to show the way.

Mrs. Chris and her friend listened attentively to the account. By the end of it they were certain that what they had seen on that strange, sweltering night was a spectral reenactment of the funeral that took place a century before.

Although there are no other well-documented sightings of the phantom funeral procession, it is said that whenever July 4th falls on a Friday, the ghostly wagons will roll out. By some accounts, there must also be a full moon in the sky. Furthermore, only three people are ever permitted to witness the event at once.

Those who wish to test the legend should take note that the next Fridays to fall on July 4 will be in the years 2003, 2014 and 2025. Look for a full moon on those nights, take two friends with you, and stake out the road between the now-restored Fort de Chartres and the old, nearby cemetery. If conditions are right, you may observe a procession of the dead, going to bury one of their own.

The Italian Bride

Death, like politics, makes strange bedfellows. Chicago's Mount Carmel Cemetery offers proof. This Italian-American burial ground is home to the Bishop's Mausoleum, within which the city's past Archdiocesan leaders are entombed, as well as the notorious gangster Al Capone and many of his crime-world cronies. Somewhere in the midst of it all lies Julia Buccola Petta, an ordinary young woman in life who became quite extraordinary after her death.

Julia was only 29 years old when she died in childbirth in 1921. It was a sad occurrence, but not uncommon at the time. Julia was laid to rest, wearing her lovely white wedding gown, in Mount Carmel Cemetery. But she refused to be forgotten.

Not long after the funeral, Julia's mother, Philomena Buccola, began to have disturbing visions and dreams in which her daughter would beg to be disinterred. For years Philomena was haunted, and for years she sought permission from the authorities for an exhumation. Finally, in 1927, permission was granted. Julia's coffin was unearthed. The lid was opened, but no one was prepared for what they saw.

The young woman's body was in immaculate condition. After six years in the ground, neither Julia nor her wedding dress showed the slightest decomposition.

A photo of the perfectly preserved body was taken. Today, it remains displayed upon the young woman's tombstone, beneath a life-sized statue of her image.

For over 70 years, the site has been a place of pilgrimage for both the curious and the pious. And those who come to feel close to Julia sometimes get more than they expect, for it is said that "the Italian Bride" wanders the grounds of Mount Carmel, eternally radiant in her flowing white wedding gown. Furthermore, one might wonder what was in her bridal bouquet, for the delicate scent of tea roses can be enjoyed frequently at her grave site—even in the winter months.

In 1927, there was proof that Julia Buccola Petta's body was surviving the grave. Today, many would say there is proof that her spirit survives, as well.

In a Rush to Rest

If ever you're driving north on Sheridan Road in Chicago, be extra alert when you pass Calvary Cemetery, at Oakton Street. For many years, there were reports of a specter who would bring traffic to a screeching halt by running across the road that separates Lake Michigan and the cemetery gates.

According to legend, the man, who apparently perished in the lake, would first be seen struggling to emerge from its cold waters. After he had pulled his dripping form up onto the rocks along the shore, he would make a desperate attempt to stagger across the road. Horns would blare and tires would squeal, but the ghost seemed oblivious to everything but his destination: Calvary Cemetery.

One version of the story tells that when the spirit reached the entrance, he would simply vanish through the iron bars. Another claims that he would encounter the closed gates and begin to pace back and forth in frustration before fading away.

This latter version also offers an explanation as to why the drowned man is rarely seen these days. It suggests that the gates of Calvary Cemetery were accidentally left unlocked one night, and that the ghost finally gained admission to his desired resting place.

Monumental Mysteries

In prehistoric times, human beings would pile stones on top of a grave, not to serve as a marker, but to protect the body from animals. As time went by, however, this practical custom evolved religious and aesthetic qualities. Modern monuments have grown so elaborate and beautiful in their honoring of the dead that they have taken on lives of their own—in more ways than one.

In Marion County, the grave of one little girl is marked with a statue of her likeness. In its delicately carved stone hands is a violin, the child's beloved instrument, and its sweet strains can often be heard throughout the cemetery.

In a cemetery in Maroa, just north of Decatur, there is a breath-taking statue of a mournful angel who is said to cry real tears. Even those who have not witnessed her actual weeping have admitted that there are some curious streaks staining her lovely stone face.

Rosehill Cemetery, in Chicago, has been home for nearly 150 years to a young mother named Frances Pearce, and her infant daughter. The two rest together below ground. Above them, their carved images recline in a peaceful sleep. To protect the lovely memorial statue of mother and daughter, a glass case was built around it. Legend now says that on the anniversaries of their deaths, the case fills with an ethereal white mist.

Further examples of supernatural stonework can be found elsewhere in Chicago, especially in Graceland Cemetery. Graceland is famous for its once-wealthy and influential residents and its collection of stunning monuments. Two of these statues have become particularly well known to the city's ghost hunters.

Monuments meant to immortalize the dead have been known to come to life.

One marks the plot of a little girl named Inez Clarke. She died in the late 19th century, leaving behind a grief-stricken family. In order to immortalize her, the girl's parents commissioned a sculpture of their lost daughter. The statue portrays the sweet child in her favorite dress, sitting daintily upon a stool with a parasol in her hands. Visitors to little Inez's grave have often been overcome by the poignant beauty of the stone figure. Somehow, the girl looks capable of rising from her perch to walk away—and there are those who say she has.

Many years ago, people began to talk about the little statue. It was reported to have gone missing one night, only to reappear in its usual spot the following morning. This occurrence is said to have happened repeatedly, until cemetery officials placed a glass box over the sculpture to prevent anyone from tampering with it. All was well for a short time. Then, late one evening, a night watchman came upon Inez Clarke's grave and discovered the impossible: the glass case was securely in position, but the statue was gone. The distraught man ran from the cemetery, leaving it unattended and unlocked.

Graceland Cemetery is also home to a monument that has been called the most chilling in Chicago. It marks the burial place of a hotelier named Dexter Graves. The statue itself has its own name, "Eternal Silence," and is also unofficially known as "the statue of Death." The looming, eight-foot-high bronze monument was sculpted in 1909 by artist Lorado Taft and has been giving people a grim glimpse of the afterlife ever since.

"Eternal Silence" is a towering, ominous figure in a draping, hooded robe. One arm is raised to obscure most of the macabre face. And, as foreboding as the statue, is the eerie legend that has become attached to it. It is said that the frightening figure so utterly defines death that it cannot be recorded by the living. In other words, it is impossible to photograph. Of course, such stories about the imposing figure have helped make it one of the most famous and most photographed monuments in the city, thus disproving the creepy theory. Like all of the mysterious monuments of Illinois, the famed "statue of Death" can be captured on film.

Misplaced Souls

You don't have to be a student of the paranormal to know that disturbing a burial ground is unwise. In every culture, these sites are considered sacred; disrupting one is believed to cause spiritual unrest, or perhaps even revenge.

So what happens when you mess with a bunch of them? What if you build an entire city over several, then move a few more around for the sake of some building permits?

Welcome to Decatur, in the heart of Illinois.

Decatur has often been described as one of the most haunted cities in the heartland, and a brief look at its history helps explain why. As the city grew, it engulfed several Native American burial sites, as well as a number of private cemeteries and small family plots. In the pioneer days, record keeping was spotty at best, and wooden markers were soon worn away by the extreme elements. Small cemeteries faded easily from sight and memory, and became lost under the streets and homes of Decatur.

Even the first official graveyards—the Common Burial Grounds and King's Cemetery—turned out to be less than permanent. The land was eventually sold to the city for subdivision, and crews began the grim task of exhuming bodies for removal to Greenwood Cemetery. But the job was never finished. For years, any construction that took place in the area seemed to unearth a new corpse. The excavation of West Main Street alone turned up literally dozens of forgotten skeletons. Even now, there is absolutely no way of knowing how many unmarked graves were steamrollered. As a result, many of the houses in that area are haunted.

One family was tormented by a troublesome spirit for years. Unable to cope with the ghost any longer, they asked a psychic to intervene. The psychic visited the home and made contact with the spirit, then gave the family some alarming news. There was a body buried under their front porch, he said. If the remains were moved, the ghost would leave. The owners of the house investigated, and, indeed, found a number of human bones buried deep beneath the porch. The anonymous remains were entrusted to city authorities and, as promised, the ghost departed.

In another home, the apparition of a wan young girl paces without rest. When she is not visible, the nearly constant sounds of whispering and knocking serve to remind the residents of her presence.

At least one home in the area is haunted, not by sight or sound, but by the terrible stench of blood.

It's true, the list of Decatur haunts is long. Among the most fascinating is Greenwood Cemetery itself. The bodies that were reburied there very likely made the cemetery one of the most haunted sites in Decatur. Over the years, countless strange stories have been told.

One woman spoke of a ghost she believes she saw there on a bright and sunny afternoon. She had gone to visit her father's grave. As she climbed a small hill in the cemetery, she noticed another woman in a black dress, holding a bouquet of yellow flowers. She was not at all far away, but in the instant that the first woman took to look down and check her footing, the lady in black disappeared. Seconds later, the astonished witness was able to survey much of the cemetery from the vantage of the hilltop, but the woman in the black dress with the yellow flowers was nowhere to be seen.

A man visiting a grave at Greenwood once encountered what can only be described as a phantom funeral party. The mourners looked so real that he kept a respectful distance, noting only that their clothes were somewhat out of date, and that they were oddly silent. The man spent no more than a few minutes placing flowers on the grave he had come to see, then began to walk back to his

The impermanence of decaying wooden markers was one reason for the loss and misidentification of so many bodies in Decatur's Greenwood Cemetery.

car. That's when he was shocked to see that the mourners had vanished. What's more, the open grave by which they had assembled was filled in—despite absolutely no sign of freshly turned earth.

Most of the spirits of Greenwood Cemetery, however, prefer to come out at night. The "Greenwood Bride" is a young woman who was so distraught following her fiancé's death that she donned her wedding dress and drowned herself in the nearby Sangamon River. She now wanders the cemetery—a glowing white vision in her gauzy gown, doomed to spend eternity searching for the spirit of her man. And she is but one of the many shadowy shapes and terrifying creatures reported by those who are brave or foolish enough to investigate Greenwood Cemetery under cover of darkness.

In the late 1970s, a Decatur man named Jack Gifford hopped the fence after sunset and was rewarded with the fright of his life. He hadn't been in the cemetery long when he saw someone not far ahead of him. Gifford, quite aware that he was trespassing, quickly hid behind a tombstone. For several minutes, he remained quiet and still, keeping his eyes on the tall, thin man's back. Gifford was certain the fellow was a cemetery caretaker, taking a careful look around the grounds. But then the stranger slowly began to turn, or, more specifically, rotate. As the man's face became visible, Gifford noted with horror that there were two empty, glowing sockets where the man's eyes should have been. No timidity with respect to trespassing could have kept Jack Gifford concealed then: he fled from Greenwood Cemetery like a thing hunted, and has never since found sufficient reason to return.

Greenwood Cemetery is also famous for its ghost lights. The ghost light is a phenomenon alternately known as "ignis fatuus" or "will-o'-the-wisp." Some cultures believed that these glowing orbs were doorways to other worlds. Science attempts to explain them away as marsh gas. In Decatur, these mysterious globes of spectral fire are believed to be the wandering souls of soldiers who were buried in Greenwood Cemetery's Civil War Memorial section.

This section is located on a hill, which has been terraced and fortified with slabs of concrete. The reinforcement took place many years ago, following a flood that left the hill and all its graves in a state of ruin. Coffins were broken, bones scattered every-where, and tombstones were lost in a huge lake of mud. The Civil War Memorial section was reassembled as best it could be, but there was no way of knowing where everything went. The result was a hopeless jumble of bones and headstones. The fact that no grave in the Civil War Memorial section of Greenwood Cemetery is guaranteed to have the right marker has given rise to a legacy of ghost lights. Darting around those mixed-up graves, they are a symbol of immortal confusion.

There is a simple lesson to be learned from the ghosts of Greenwood Cemetery. The dead do not like to be disturbed. Treat them respectfully, and always allow them to rest in peace.

The Joliet Crooner

Late one summer evening in 1932, a fisherman from Joliet was walking home with his day's catch. The man decided to take a shortcut through the potter's field that belonged to Joliet Prison. The fisherman meant only to save a little time, but ended up with a story he would never forget.

As he walked across the cemetery, he heard a voice in the darkness. "Any luck today?" it inquired. The man turned to respond to the friendly question, and was startled to see no one behind him. He spun around, searching for another human being, but found himself utterly alone. The disembodied voice then began to sing something low and lovely, in a foreign language. The fisherman opted not to stay for the impromptu performance, and ran as fast as he could across the graveyard. He did not know it at the time, but he was among the first of thousands who would witness the singing ghost of Joliet Prison.

Others who heard the phantom voice early on didn't know what they were listening to. During the summer, people in the neighboring residential area would often sit outside all evening. When they began hearing the beautiful baritone singing Latin hymns, each presumed to be listening to another's radio. Eventually, the people living closest to the prison realized that the potter's field was the source of the music. Word spread, and crowds began to gather nightly to hear the singing ghost.

As the story became common knowledge, people came from all over to hear the ghost's hymns. Lines of cars brought in hundreds and eventually thousands of curious spectators. They brought blankets to sit on, picnic lunches and thermoses of hot coffee or flasks of something a little stronger. Most wished simply to experience the ghost, but some came hoping to debunk it.

Whenever the spirit began to sing—usually around midnight—some members of the audience would spring into action, determined to track down the source. They searched for wires, speakers and microphones, but never found any. They would try to follow the dulcet music, but were frustrated because, while it was always nearby, it was never exactly where anyone was standing. Bushes and trees were searched, but nothing was found. In the end, even the skeptics had to consider that they might be listening to an actual phantom.

After a few weeks, the ghost began to arrive late for his midnight "curtain call." Then there were nights when the lovely baritone was not heard at all. Eventually, it became clear that the spectral show was over—and the speculation began in earnest.

The official word was that a practical joker had been discovered. He was an inmate of the Joliet Prison, a convict named William Chrysler, who had been given the unpleasant task of checking the sump pumps in the limestone quarry near the cemetery at night. Chrysler claimed that the "Latin hymns" people heard were actually Lithuanian folk songs he sang to fend off boredom as he worked in the quarry, and added that when he discovered what a fuss he was causing, he actually altered the songs a bit to make them sound more religious. Prison officials announced that the rock walls were acoustically responsible for throwing the prisoner's voice more than a quarter of a mile to the potter's field. After this explanation was given, the authorities announced that the case was closed.

The people, however, continued to talk. The authorities' rational explanation seemed more incredible than the ghostly phenomenon itself. William Chrysler would not have been working down in the quarry without a light, but no light was ever seen by the countless spectators in the cemetery, including those who had searched for an explanation. And how could it be that the quarry walls transported the sound of Chrysler's singing, but not the sound of the noisy sump pumps that he was supposedly maintaining?

It is entirely feasible that prison officials simply tired of the endless trespassing, and, once the strange singing had stopped, contrived an end to the hubbub. As for William Chrysler, he wasn't going to contradict their story—he was eligible for parole within days.

So why did the ghost stop singing? Around the time the "official explanation" was released, a Roman Catholic priest supposedly performed an exorcism at the potter's field. Perhaps that was enough to let the spectral soloist rest in peace. The beautiful voice that fired so many imaginations during that warm July has been silent ever since.

Miracles and Roses

Mary Alice Quinn was a devout young Roman Catholic who emulated St. Theresa of Lisieux. Like Theresa, Mary Alice expressed her devotion through daily acts of kindness—some simple, and some simply beyond explanation. The girl was said to have had healing powers, and allegedly cured several people of their ailments during her lifetime. Sadly, that lifetime was short: Mary Alice Quinn was buried at the tender age of 14.

Many who have visited her grave in Chicago's Holy Sepulchre Cemetery say that her miraculous work continues. Since her death in 1935, countless pilgrims have traveled to Mary Alice's grave. After praying for her help, many have walked away declaring themselves cured of illness or injury. Others leave with a handful of the sacred soil, wanting to take the miracle home with them. Her renown as a healer has only grown since her passing, causing her to become known as "Chicago's Miracle Child."

One sign of Mary Alice Quinn's spiritual presence at her grave is the powerful smell of roses. It can be experienced at any time of year, and is often so overwhelming that visitors find they have to walk away from it. A rose in any form has always been a sign to Roman Catholics that a prayer has been answered by Mary Alice's chosen patron, St. Theresa.

St. James of the Sag

St. James of the Sag is one of the most restless cemeteries in Illinois. It lies adjacent to St. James Church on Archer Avenue, the same road which Resurrection Mary loves to travel. The locals know it simply as St. James-Sag.

The church and burial ground date back to the 1830s, and reports of ghostly activity date back as far as 1847, when spectral monks were first seen skimming soundlessly across the grounds. The monks have remained a haunting fixture, sometimes appearing as shadowy, hooded figures, and sometimes heard filling the air with the mysterious sound of Gregorian chant. One particularly credible account was reported in November 1977. A Cook County sheriff who was passing the cemetery one night saw eight figures in dark robes gliding from the woods toward the rectory. When the sheriff attempted to pursue them, they simply turned—and vanished.

There have been stories of other types of paranormal phenomena over the years, as well. One pastor maintained that he would often look out over the cemetery and see the ground swelling and receding in rhythmic waves. Others spoke of a phantom ball of light that would dance among the graves.

But the most intriguing of all the legends of St. James-Sag actually begins at another burial ground on Archer Avenue—Resurrection Cemetery.

For years, there were frightening tales told of a spectral horse-drawn hearse that would come bolting out of the gates of Resurrection Cemetery and tear madly down Archer Avenue. The wild-eyed horses would be panting; the driver, conspicuously absent. As the beasts raced to escape some unseen terror, horrified witnesses would only have a moment to view the hearse's cargo. Within the ornate black oak and glass carriage lay a small, glowing object. It was the casket of a child.

After some time, people began to suspect that the mysterious hearse was not the exclusive property of Resurrection Cemetery, for an identical apparition had often been seen at a different point on Archer Avenue. It was called the "Sag Bridge Ghost," and was very likely the same vehicle, farther along its route.

In September 1897, two unsuspecting musicians were witness to the conclusion of the hearse's journey.

The young men, William Looney and John Kelly, had been hired to play the harp and flute at a church fundraiser. The two fellows spent an enjoyable but exhausting evening performing in a dance hall that was just a short walk from St. James Church. At the end of the night, they were too tired to travel back into Chicago and decided instead to sleep in a couple of cots that were kept on the upper floor of the hall.

It was after 1 AM when the men settled in. Kelly fell asleep immediately, but Looney found himself restless and unable to doze off. He was lying awake, studying the patterns of moonlight and shadow on the ceiling, when there was a sudden clamor outside. Looney could hear horses' hooves pounding on the ground, and the thunderous sound of a heavy carriage. Wondering who would be in such a hurry in the wee hours of the morning, Looney jumped up to look out the window. He saw nothing.

The noise increased steadily, as though the team and carriage were growing closer to the dance hall, yet nothing was visible in the moonlight. After a moment, the strange sound ceased. William Looney returned to his cot, where he sat, bewildered and afraid. It was only a few minutes before he decided to wake his friend.

As Looney told Kelly about the bizarre experience, it started to happen again. The roaring commotion of the horses and carriage was heard clearly by both men this time, but still no trace of them could be seen.

As the two stood staring out the window, they were stunned by the sudden appearance of a ghost—one wholly unrelated to the pounding hooves. A tall woman with wild, dark hair and a white gown had materialized in the middle of the road. Her face was contorted in an expression of misery and she was frantically waving, as though some desperate emergency were at hand. The woman appeared so very real that the two men were about to call out to her, when suddenly she turned, melted through the cemetery fence and began walking aimlessly among the graves.

At that point, the phantom carriage could be heard again— and, this time, the ominous sound was accompanied by an incredible image. Looney and Kelly saw two white horses. A lacy network of filaments stretched across their hides, and from their foreheads shone beams of incandescent light. The men had time to take a good look at the vehicle that the horses were drawing as well, and saw that it was no ordinary carriage. Dark, ponderous and solemn, it seemed the perfect conveyance for death itself. No driver sat atop it.

The sound of the approaching vehicle drew the dark-haired woman back to the road. As the phantom coach passed her, she seemed to be enveloped by a shadow, and then she disappeared. The team and carriage also vanished, but not for long. Moments later, the deafening sound began once more, and the woman reappeared. As the spectral transport passed her for the second time, she screamed out, "Come on!" No sooner had the woman uttered the words, than she was swallowed up by the road. The team and carriage followed suit. Suddenly, all was quiet, as though the woman and the horses had never been there at all.

Looney and Kelly dared not move until daybreak. When the sun finally dispelled the gloom of night, they decided to pay a visit to the local police. As strange as their tale was, their sincere and sober testimony convinced the authorities.

As for explanations? There is one story, from the 1880s, about a pastor's assistant who fell in love with one of the housekeepers from the rectory. The lovers decided to elope, but were tragically killed when their horses reared and the carriage in which they were meant to escape overturned and crushed them. It is said they were buried together in an unmarked plot, just a short distance from where they died. This story, however, leaves many questions about the ghosts unanswered. If the woman's fiancé was coming to collect her, why was the carriage without a driver? And why would the vehicle be racing all the way from Resurrection Cemetery?

What William Looney and John Kelly saw on that strange September night may never be explained. It must simply be accepted as part of the mystery of St. James-Sag.

Chapter 6

HAUNTED HOUSES

When a spirit remains on this plane of
existence in order to continue the routines of its life,
the place it is most likely to inhabit is its former home.
What most ghosts are insensitive to is the fact that
their home has now become someone else's castle—
and therein lies the conflict.

Encountering a specter in a public place might
be unnerving, but having one as a roommate is much
worse. Our homes are places of refuge and comfort.
Having a resident ghost seldom adds to one's
sense of security.

Even those who don't believe in spirits
will speak of houses having a good or bad "vibe."
If the very walls of a building can be imprinted with
emotions and memories, is it such a stretch of
imagination to think that departed residents might
also linger? In many cases, it appears that they do.

The following are several classic accounts of
haunted houses in Illinois.

Hickory Hill Slave House

The two men were Marines, members of America's finest fighting force. They had seen combat in Vietnam—bloodshed and horror unimaginable to most—and they had never backed down. But now, in the early morning hours, they were running from a fight for the first time in their lives. Desperate and terrified, they fled down the narrow wooden stairs with hearts pounding. They burst out the door and gasped in the cool, sweet night air, but did not stop. Nor did they stop when they reached the safety of their vehicle, slamming and locking the doors and fumbling in a panic to fit the key into the ignition. In fact, the knots of fear in their chests only began to loosen a little when they had put several miles behind them. They would never return to collect their abandoned gear.

The horror the Marines had faced that night was not found in a foreign jungle, but in a historic house in southern Illinois. There were stories about the place. It was said that many had tried to endure a night in its third-floor attic, and that none had been successful. To the Marines, that had sounded like a challenge. They had volunteered their time, certain that the worst they would suffer would be a few hours of boredom.

They had settled into the attic, which was a bleak, gray, wooden space divided into tiny cells, with a main corridor. The dim, yellow glow from a single kerosene lantern had cast long shadows into the room. After a couple of uneventful hours, the Marines had thought they might catch some sleep. Just then, the lantern began to flicker. As one of the men reached over to adjust it, a sudden sound pierced the dusty air. The cry was unearthly, a shrieking moan that voiced some unspeakable agony. Frozen with fear, the Marines listened as other disembodied voices joined in. High-pitched screams surrounded them. Low, sinister voices muttered unintelligibly from the deep shadows. When those shadows began to writhe, taking shape into dozens of ghostly forms, survival instinct kicked in. As the entities advanced upon them, the Marines ran. And so it was, in 1966, that two members of the most elite branch of the United States Armed Forces were overcome by terror. They added their names to a long list of people who had been unable to spend a night in the attic of the Old Slave House, the most haunted house in Illinois, and the most graphic relic of a shameful past.

On July 27, 1829, the following item appeared in the news:

HORRID OUTRAGE! Was Kidnapped, in the neighborhood of the Saline, a NEGRO GIRL, named MARIA, about eight years of age, dark complexion, nearly black, well grown of her age. She was taken from the spring on Saturday evening of the 25th by two ruffians who are unknown. This girl is one of the Negroes emancipated by the last will and testament of John McAilister.

The article was written by Leo D. White for a newspaper in the small community of Equality, Illinois. Although people of the largely black settlement were surely outraged, the sad fact was that such kidnappings in Southern Illinois had become commonplace. Freed slaves who had settled in the state were often snatched by cruel bands of nightriders who called themselves "Regulators." They were then smuggled across state lines to be resold into servitude. The Regulators were one component of the disgraceful, but highly organized, network of criminals known as the Reverse Underground Railroad.

The Reverse Underground Railroad provided many people in the southern counties of Illinois with a tidy income for very little risk. While it certainly was illegal, the offense of kidnapping and reselling freed slaves was nearly impossible to prosecute. For the charge to stick, the prosecutor had to prove that the victim had been taken across state lines—a nearly impossible task, particularly since, at that time, blacks could not testify against whites in a court of law.

Because this profitable crime was so easy to commit, and because many whites in Southern Illinois sympathized with the South, some of the worst offenders were "upstanding" members of the community. The fact is, while poor little Maria's family and neighbors scrambled to raise a reward for her return, the girl was very likely being held in a tiny attic cell above one of the finest homes in Gallatin County. The grand building sat high atop wind-swept Hickory Hill, and was known then as the Crenshaw Mansion. Decades later, it would be remembered as the Old Slave House.

Nowadays, there are sudden icy breezes in that gray attic prison, even when the windows are sealed shut. There are those who have heard the sounds of suffering there—whimpering, crying, ghostly moaning. The wooden floorboards whisper with the sound of bare feet shuffling across them, and one can easily imagine fingers curled desperately around the iron bars of the cell windows that face the hallway. Painful memories haunt the makeshift prison, memories of torments endured, memories of the terrible man who inflicted them.

John Hart Crenshaw was born on November 19, 1797, into a respectable American family. His grandfather, John Hart, was a signatory to the Declaration of Independence. Some bad financial luck and the early death of Crenshaw's father meant that the young man started out in poverty, and had to rely on his wits to make a living. He soon found opportunities that would reward his cunning.

Although Illinois was technically a free state, there were three forms of slavery that were recognized: French slaves and their descendants, allowed under the 1783 Treaty of Paris; indentured servants; and slaves that were leased from other states to labor in the salt works in Gallatin, Hardin and Saline Counties. When Crenshaw learned of the last group, he saw his chance to get ahead. He quickly leased a number of salt springs from the government, and made arrangements with slaveholders in Kentucky and Tennessee to provide the labor. The plan worked. Within a few years, Crenshaw was so wealthy that he alone paid one-seventh of the total taxes collected in the state. The profit wasn't enough to satisfy the man's greed, however. John Crenshaw wanted more. As he watched the slaves toiling in his mines and fields, the man who had come to be known as the "Salt King" realized that he might be looking at something even more profitable than salt.

Slaves who had worked in Crenshaw's mines and earned enough to buy their freedom became his next commodity. Working with a band of highly trustworthy and loyal accomplices, Crenshaw began to kidnap black men, women and children. He spirited them across state lines and auctioned them as slaves in the South. There was little interference from the law or the public, because attitudes in Southern Illinois at that time reflected widespread sympathy for the South. Proof of a state bitterly divided on the issue of slavery can be found in one 1851 issue of the Shawneetown Gazette, in which Chicago is referred to as a "sinkhole of abolitionism."

There were many involved in the terrible business of trafficking slaves, but Crenshaw quickly became the most notorious. He enjoyed his crimes so much that he built his house with them in mind. Construction of Crenshaw's dream house began in 1834.

On the outside, it dwarfed all other buildings in sight with its plantation-style grandeur and its Grecian pillars. On the inside, it was a labyrinth of passageways. There was an enclosed drive-way within the walls of the house, so that carriages carrying kidnapped slaves could be loaded and unloaded away from prying eyes. It was rumored that the house was also connected by a tunnel to the Saline River, where waiting boats would be loaded with the human cargo. Worst of all, there was the attic, a prison composed of cells no larger than horse stalls. Indeed, Crenshaw treated his prisoners no better than breeding livestock. Iron rings, to which the prisoners were chained, were bolted to the floor of each cramped chamber. In the corridor, there were whipping posts, and heavy, metal shackles—many in sizes small enough for children. The design of the house allowed John Crenshaw to conduct his horrible business in utter secrecy.

Only a few feet beneath the horror of the attic, the Crenshaws lived as upstanding Christians and pillars of the community. The children attended school, the family supported the Equality Methodist Church and John Crenshaw operated a number of legitimate businesses. He also served on several public boards and commissions. Although there is evidence that Crenshaw was not loved by his neighbors, he was powerful enough to command a certain measure of respect. Not only was Crenshaw wealthy, but he also wielded political clout. Ironically, the Great Emancipator, Abraham Lincoln, was an overnight guest at the Crenshaw home in September 1840, following a week of debates in Gallatin County.

Although Lincoln likely had no knowledge of the horrors that were happening above his head, Crenshaw's actions weren't going entirely unnoticed. The local courts were growing suspicious. He was twice indicted on kidnapping charges—in 1825 and 1842—but never convicted.

The fact is, historians were not able to offer proof of Crenshaw's illegal operation until more than a century after his death. It took years for suspicion and rumor to congeal into fact. Nor were Crenshaw's descendants much help in solving the mystery. They were from the beginning divided into two camps. Some handed down stories about a cruel man whose weapon of choice for punishing workers was a branding iron, and who forced his children to watch when he whipped the slaves. Others maintained that Crenshaw had been kind, misunderstood and envied. The latter group even attempted to explain the existence of the attic cells by suggesting that they were a stop on the Underground Railroad to freedom. Why that stop would have required iron shackles and barred windows, they didn't say. Nor could they explain the residual sensation of utter anguish.

By the mid-1840s, Crenshaw's massive empire was beginning to crumble. Just before he stood trial for kidnapping in 1842, arsonists burned his steam mill to the ground. A few years later, he lost a leg—in a sawmill accident according to some accounts, at the hands of a furious, ax-wielding slave according to others. The slaves were becoming more mutinous, which made Crenshaw's operation of the mines more difficult. Moreover, rich salt deposits that had been discovered in Virginia and Ohio put an end to the Illinois Salt King's virtual monopoly. Weary of the legal and economic battles, he eventually retired to farming. On December 4, 1871, the "good Methodist" who once named a favorite horse "Prince Lucifer" went to his final trial. That last court did not release him.

The Crenshaw house stayed in the Crenshaw family until 1906, when it was purchased by a man named Sisk. By the 1920s, there was considerable interest in the notorious building, and Mr. Sisk had numerous people knocking on his door and asking for tours. In 1930, he and his wife officially opened the house to the public and began charging admission—a nickel for children, a dime for adults. An unforeseen and interesting effect resulted from the Sisks' new enterprise: the more people that ventured into the attic, the more strange stories they came down with. On top of being a site of historical interest, the Old Slave House was fast gaining a reputation for being haunted.

Tourists often came downstairs, ashen and shaking, reporting sensations of extreme discomfort, dread, and fright. The Sisks noted that the overwhelming emotional reactions of the visitors went beyond the expected empathetic response to the tragic site. Some people claimed to have glimpsed shadowy, swirling forms in the corners, and felt pockets of icy air that chilled them to the bone on the most sweltering of summer days. Others heard baleful cries, and the unmistakable rattling of chains.

Two generations later, grandson George Sisk II and his wife Janice continued to operate their family home as a tourist attraction. They also continued to collect stories of mysterious experiences that people had in their attic. One woman was so distressed, she forced the Sisks to follow her back upstairs, where she showed them how, in a number of locations in the attic, the hair on her arms would stand on end. Other tourists complained of being constantly watched when, of course, they were actually quite alone. One educated and pragmatic man, a professor at a university in Chicago, could not shake the sensation of being observed while he toured the Old Slave House attic. Although he knew he was alone, the feeling was so strong that he found himself looking over his shoulder several times. As he viewed the scarred wooden walls, and the remains of the cruel shackles and chains, his discomfort grew. Finally, he left, feeling relief wash over him as he climbed into his car, which was parked on the front driveway. Before pulling away, the professor turned to take one last look at the attic window—and froze. There, behind the glass, was a face staring out at him. The apparition lasted a few seconds, then vanished. The professor went directly back into the house to ask George Sisk if anyone else had gone up to the attic. The answer was no; Sisk was alone in the house, and had been on the main floor.

Over the years, George and Janice Sisk have become accustomed to such questions. And although they rarely venture into the attic themselves, they have their own inexplicable stories. Janice Sisk has spoken of being frequently unnerved by the strange sounds of the house. Some, she says, she can explain away, but others she cannot. One night as she lay in bed, there was a tremendous hammering beneath the floorboards. On several other evenings, while alone in the house and taking a bath, she would clearly hear her name called out. The voice was so real that she thought her husband had come home early. Now she refuses to get into the tub unless he is home. Janice Sisk has also mentioned seeing fleeting forms out of the corner of her eye, and says that both she and her husband feel constantly observed while they are in the house. Their son, George III, feels it necessary to hang a rosary on his dresser, "to keep the devil out" of his room. At the beginning of her marriage, Janice Sisk felt so threatened by the house that she actually left for a period of time. Now, however, both husband and wife live peacefully with their spectral roommates. In fact, in 1998, after surveying the damage of the second burglary at the house, Janice Sisk told reporter Jon Musgrave, "As I've told people before, it's not the ones upstairs I'm worried about. It's the live ones outside."

There are many who don't agree that the forces in the Old Slave House are harmless. 150 people, including the two U.S. Marines, attempted, and failed, to spend a single night in the dreadful attic. Finally, in 1978, a reporter named David Rodgers endured an entire night in the attic. Comparatively speaking, he'd had an easy time of it— yet Rodgers still claimed to be exhausted from doing battle with his fear, and declared that he didn't want to repeat the adventure soon.

David Rodgers's reaction is understandable; after all, some even say the Old Slave House has killed. Newspaper clippings from the late 1920s describe an exorcist named Hickman Whittington who attempted to do battle with the spirits of the Old Slave House. Whittington was in excellent health when he entered the house. Within hours, he was dead. Decades later, George Sisk opined that Hickman Whittington died of fright. Perhaps that is why the Sisks have turned down several offers to have the house cleansed of its spirits. George Sisk has gone on to say that the ghosts can have the attic to themselves. Their continuing existence is a tribute to the terrible suffering that occurred there.

It was suffering that left an indelible psychic mark upon the attic, scarring its atmosphere as surely as the iron rings and shackles that were once bolted to the floors and walls have left tell-tale scars upon the wood. Today, the Old Slave House stands as a reminder of a time that we must never be allowed to forget. The ghosts, enduring their torment into eternity, ensure that we never will.

Voorhies Castle

A few miles south of Monticello, in east-central Illinois, lie the remains of the tiny town of Voorhies. It was never a metropolis, but these days Voorhies doesn't even register on the map. It consists of a couple of abandoned buildings, the odd house and an aged mansion known as Voorhies Castle.

In its day, Voorhies Castle was famous among ghost hunters, and was considered to be the most haunted house in Central Illinois. Stories about the place were so plentiful and convincing that a parapsychology group from the University of Illinois conducted an investigation. Renowned psychic Irene Hughes once visited the castle as well, and felt unable to spend more than a moment inside it. Voorhies Castle was so notorious that when it was open to tourists in the late 1960s, it attracted more than 30,000 visitors annually.

Today, its reputation has faded. The grand old home has become a private residence where the ghost stories are vehemently denied and inquisitive trespassers are unwelcome. There are no recent reports of strange activity. But whether or not there is anything paranormal about Voorhies Castle today, its ghostly history is too fascinating to be forgotten.

The Castle was built around the beginning of the 20th century by a Swedish immigrant named Nels Larson. Larson was a hard worker, and smart with his money. Nearly all his earnings were invested in real estate, and within a few years Larson owned a sizable farm and the entire town of Voorhies. He then set about having a home built for his wife Johanna. He intended that it reflect his importance in the community.

An impressive 14-room Swedish manor house was the result. Fitted with such luxurious details as Tiffany glass windows,

Voorhies Castle cost more than $9000—a considerable amount at the time. There was even a room built as a sort of studio for Johanna, who was quite talented with the paintbrush. Nels and Johanna Larson moved into their magnificent new home, and started a family.

For years, the Larsons lived in Voorhies Castle. During their time there, the first of many strange stories began to be told. It was said that one of the Larson children was born with such severe mental and physical handicaps that it was never taken out of the house. Worse, rumor claimed that the Larsons had built a secret room within their home, and that the child was kept there, cruelly chained to the wall. The stories may have begun in the overactive imaginations of townsfolk who envied the Larsons' wealth—or they may have had a grain of truth. At that time, a less-than-perfect child would certainly have harmed the couple's social standing, so hiding it would have been desirable. Although confining a child to its room with chains is obviously inhumane, many worse "treatments" were applied to the mentally ill in the early 1900s. Years later, those who visited Voorhies Castle said that the metallic rattling of chains could still be heard coming from some unknown space behind the walls.

In 1914, Johanna Larson died—quite suddenly and unexpectedly. A field hand discovered her, one afternoon, collapsed in a heap on the floor. It was assumed, but never determined for certain, that she had suffered a heart attack while descending the stairs.

Nels Larson was overcome with shock and grief—and dealt with the situation in a very strange manner. He gathered his children and left Voorhies Castle that very night, never to return. For years, the house sat unoccupied, displaying evidence of the Larsons' sudden departure. Clothes hung in the closets. Toys were scattered on the floor. The furniture stood ready to be used, including the dining room table, which had been set for dinner. In all of the silent rooms, there was a sense that something very unusual was present.

Indeed, many people who trespassed onto the Larson property for a peek at the abandoned luxury saw more than they expected. After dark, it was reported that a spooky light could be seen glowing in the window of the west tower. There, the silhouette of a woman could be seen, sitting at an easel.

Nels Larson died in 1923, and left behind a will stating that the house was to remain in the family. None of Larson's heirs wanted to live in Voorhies Castle, however; for some reason, it had been built with every luxury except electricity. The home was rented out but was destined to recurring periods of vacancy. No one tenant ever stayed for long. Meanwhile, the eerie stories accumulated.

Accompanying the tales of clanking chains and a phantom artist were other chilling details. One caretaker of the house complained that securely locked windows would open on their own, and that he would see lights emanating defiantly from certain rooms, after he had extinguished them. There were stories of a heavy marble plant stand that would spin around in its place on the floor so frequently that the carpet and wood were worn away. It was said that someone in the house had died of fright on a sofa, and that the imprint of the body could not be removed from the upholstery. Furthermore, locals maintained that a clock tower built in the barn would chime 13 times on the anniversary of Nels Larson's death. The tower was destroyed in a tornado in 1976, but many say that the clock continues to issue its somber anniversary toll.

The stately house did eventually leave the Larson family's hands, and the current owners are attempting to restore both its beauty and its reputation. They are enjoying some success, for over the last 25 years, there has been a loss of interest in the house, and an apparent decline in paranormal activity. Is it possible that whatever once possessed Voorhies Castle has moved on?

Psychic Irene Hughes once had the following to say about the home: "What we have in this house is an entity that is stuck in time. People just need to forget this thing and let it pass on."

Perhaps it has.

The Stickney Mansion

In the tiny village of Bull Valley, in McHenry County, sits the unique Stickney Mansion. To describe it in one sentence would be a challenge, but a man who spent several years contemplating the mansion from his own house, across the street, once met that challenge with this succinct description: "It gives you the feeling that it's alive," he said.

The two-story English country house is a strange sight in the village: it has arched windows, wood porticos and a tawny brick exterior. But the home's most unusual feature is somewhat less obvious.

The mansion was built in the 1840s to the eccentric specifications of George and Sylvia Stickney. The couple insisted that their secluded home should have no right angles. The Stickneys had their reasons for insisting upon the architectural peculiarity— they were avid spiritualists who believed, as did many at that time, that spirits could get trapped in square corners. Since they planned on conducting many a seance within their mansion, they definitely did not want it to be a ghost trap. As a result, the strange house was built with its curious angles and rounded edges.

The mansion soon became a popular gathering place for those who sought communication with the dead. The Stickneys held seances regularly in the huge second-floor ballroom, and Sylvia Stickney achieved a reputation as a talented medium. Spirits weren't the only visitors, however. The couple was famous for its hospitality toward the living. The Stickneys opened their home as a guest house to Civil War soldiers, and entertained them with the music of the county's first piano.

The Stickneys had created the perfect environment for their lifestyle—but one error had been made. In the home that was meant to have no square corners, there was a single 90-degree angle. The architect and builders likely considered it no more than a minor oversight, but it proved fatal. For it was in that one room, with the one corner, that George Stickney was one day found dead. There was no apparent cause.

In the 1960s, a group of hippies took up residence in Stickney mansion. They painted the rooms in funereal, dark colors, built open fires right in the middle of the floors, and spray-painted offensive slogans and images on the walls. Eventually they moved on, leaving behind a variety of drug paraphernalia, evidence of satanic rituals and some newly awakened spirits.

A man named Rodrick Smith lived in Stickney Mansion for a portion of the 1970s. When he left, he claimed that ghosts had made the place uninhabitable. Smith's dogs constantly barked for no apparent reason, and there were strange, whispering voices heard in all of the rooms.

Subsequent tenants lived with the proliferating ghost stories, whether they agreed with them or not. In a photo taken for real estate purposes, two images could be seen in the arched windows of the mansion: the photo showed a veiled woman in a wedding gown, and a butler pulling back the draperies with white-gloved hands. The photographer steadfastly maintained that the mansion had been vacant at the time the picture was taken.

Other stories tell of a shadowy shape that would lurk about the ballroom. Most pervasive of all was the discomforting feeling visitors had of being constantly watched, no matter where they were on the property. "The entire grounds of the Stickney Estate are electric with this feeling," wrote Dylan Clearfield, in his 1997 book, *Chicagoland Ghosts.*

Stickney Mansion is now owned by the Village of Bull Valley, and serves as the local police headquarters. Village officials scoff at the idea that the place is, or ever was, haunted, saying that such rumors spread when the house was vacant and frequently targeted by vandals.

Still, there are those—like the neighbor across the street—who maintain that the building is alive with spiritual energy. If only George and Sylvia Stickney were here to tell us for sure.

The Faceless Gray Phantom

On June 26, 1923, a retired coal miner named Jacob Meyer had an early lunch, retired to his favorite chair, put a .32 caliber revolver to his temple and pulled the trigger. The local paper announced that Meyer had been "found dead in chair by wife, bullet through his brain." It went on to explain that the 77-year-old man had been despondent because of ill health. Meyer's wife moved away, the house was sold, and, like the weathered words on an old grave, the story of Jacob Meyer's death gradually faded from memory.

In 1956, Dollie and Judy Walta bought a two-story brick house on Main Street in Belleville, Illinois. The purchase was the culmination of a dream they had nurtured for years: finally, they were able to open their own music studio. The women moved their instruments in, and set up shop. For several years, all was calm. They taught their lessons and noticed nothing out of the ordinary. But in 1962, they undertook a few renovations. Making changes to an old home often stirs up spiritual activity and, one evening, as Judy entered the dark, empty house through the back door, she was greeted by a ghost. It was a white, misty form in the shape of a human, the first of many paranormal encounters Dollie and Judy would have in their studio.

Later that same year, a friend of the Waltas named Jim Bawling drowned. The day after his funeral, the two women distinctly sensed his presence in the room where they had enjoyed his last visit. As if to confirm the sensation, a pencil that had belonged to Bawling rolled up a slanted desktop, then maneuvered to point at the chair where the young man had always sat.

Thereafter, the sisters were frequently visited by their departed friend. They would hear the back door opening by itself, and listen to the familiar footsteps coming down the hall. If they happened to be in the room that contained Bawling's favorite chair, they would actually hear him sit down in it. It was unnerving at first, but gradually the women grew accustomed to Bawling's visits, and would greet him with a casual "Hello, Jim," before carrying on with their work.

Just as Dollie and Judy Walta were becoming comfortable with these visits to their studio, they began to notice phantom footsteps that obviously did not belong to Jim Bawling. Bawling's tread was light and confident; the unfamiliar gait was heavy and lumbering.

One afternoon in March 1966, the sisters were tending to chores in different rooms, both off the main hall. At exactly 1:20, both women looked up to witness the same astonishing sight. A fairly tall, thickset man in drab, gray clothing was standing in the hall. Where his face should have been, there was nothing but a gray blur. The man's other notable feature was his slight transparency—Dollie Walta was stunned to realize that as she looked at him, she could see directly into the room across the hall. The gray man walked away without a sound. Each sister felt that he had been looking directly at her.

The spirit of Jim Bawling stopped appearing at that time, and the strange new ghost became a frequent visitor. The Waltas had always tried to keep the studio's paranormal quirks a secret from students, but that became impossible as more and more bizarre experiences occurred. One skeptical fellow had his belief system altered when he saw a toilet in the house flushing violently and inexplicably. A female student felt an icy hand on her back. It was so realistic that she could distinguish each individual finger. Some would smell cigar smoke when the windows were closed and no one was smoking in the building, and others reported the scraping sounds of a chair being dragged across the floor. A group of four people once witnessed a dancing umbrella, and many heard the mysterious sounds of a door opening and closing, followed by heavy, disembodied footsteps moving down the hall. Worst of all, when the Walta sisters were locking up one night, they distinctly heard a gunshot from within the studio.

Worried that their uninvited guest might be scaring off potential clients, Judy Walta began to do a little research. After several trips to the local library, she finally found an item of interest, namely, the newspaper article from June 1923 that reported Jacob Meyer's suicide. The death had occurred in Meyer's home, the two-story brick house on Main Street in Belleville, Illinois.

Judy took the information home to Dollie, and the two mused over whether Jacob Meyer could be their ghost in gray. Was the spirit unable to show his face because, following his gruesome suicide, he had none left to show? Or was he hiding his face in shame because he died by his own hand, which was considered at the time to be an act of extreme cowardice?

The Walta sisters would never know, but ultimately it did not matter. Once they identified their faceless specter, the strange activity began to taper off. The more they discussed Jacob Meyer's reason for being there, the less he was there, until, one day, the studio could hardly be considered haunted at all.

Haunted on Old Homestead Road

Encountering a ghost, or anything else paranormal, is always unsettling. That which is unfamiliar makes us afraid, although it might be quite benign or even friendly. Imagine, then, the terror one would feel when dealing with a spirit that clearly meant you harm. One Illinois family doesn't have to imagine it. They lived it.

Rod and Angela Burns and their daughter Crystal (all pseudonyms) moved into a ranch house on an acreage on Old Homestead Road in St. Charles in 1981. In appearance, the three-bedroom home was far from the typical haunted house. There was no attic for rattling chains, no basement full of dark shadows and secret passageways. Furthermore, the home had no unsavory history: it was only a few years old. For the Burns, the house seemed perfect. There was even a small barn out back, which was ideal for the animal-loving family. Rod and Angela planned to add a few chickens and rabbits to their collection of pets.

The Burns settled into their new home and into a regular routine. All seemed well for a short time. Then, one quiet afternoon when she was alone in the house, Angela decided to take a long, hot bath. She was relaxing in the tub, when suddenly she heard loud footsteps in the hall. Rod was at work, Crystal was at school, and the family dog had not made a sound to announce anyone's arrival. Feeling vulnerable and afraid, Angela quickly wrapped herself in a robe and ventured out of the bathroom. She somehow found the courage to check the entire house, but there was no evidence of anyone having been there. The first of many inexplicable incidents had occurred.

After that, footsteps were frequently heard in the Burns home, as were mysterious music and other sounds. Crashing noises were often heard in one bedroom or another, but when Rod and Angela would investigate, nothing would ever be out of place. Lights began to turn themselves on and off, and no matter how securely anyone shut a door or window, there was no guarantee it would stay shut. The Burns family was forced to realize that it was not alone in the house.

By the time the family had been living on Old Homestead Road six months, the ghostly hostility had escalated. Angela began to have the most horrible nightmares of her life. Night after night, terrifying images would invade her sleep. They were often ghastly scenarios in which she and her daughter were butchered and eaten. Young Crystal's rest was disturbed, as well: she told her parents that there were shadowy figures swooping around her bedroom at night, and insisted upon putting a crucifix and a bottle of holy water by the bed for protection. House guests weren't spared, either. Angela's visiting brother spent one night in the spare room, and was awakened by invisible hands shaking the bed. Her father tried napping in the same bed, and was shaken awake and told to leave. In his semiconscious state, he thought it was his wife who had roused him. Minutes later, he was shocked to discover that she had never been in the room.

Although many people experienced strange things in the house, Angela was most frequently targeted, and seemed especially attuned to the malevolent atmosphere. She was the only one to ever see a ghost there—she encountered a dense white mist on several occasions—and her horrible dreams were sometimes premonitory. In one nightmare, Angela foresaw the death of their cat. Within days, it happened. The Burns family buried their pet alongside the parakeets, canaries, chickens and rabbits that had died during the family's short time on the acreage.

In exasperation, Angela decided one day to consult a psychic. Although Angela provided her with no specific details, the woman was alarmingly accurate in naming the problem. "Your house is cursed," she said, bluntly. "And, in particular, the spirits do not like you." Angela's suspicions were confirmed: the ghosts were singling her out.

The stress of living in a haunted abode, along with the fact that Angela was much more affected by it than Rod, began to take its toll. Husband and wife found themselves fighting frequently, and the arguments began to escalate. During one particularly terrible screaming match, Angela threw a telephone at Rod. It missed its mark, hurtling instead through a large plate-glass window. Angela ran from the room in tears, and Rod followed. A few minutes later, in a calmer state, the couple returned to inspect the damage. They were both stunned to find none. The telephone sat in its usual spot, there wasn't a splinter of glass to be found, and the window was in one piece. Not long after that, Angela moved out of the house, taking Crystal with her. With their marriage in near ruins, and a nearly uninhabitable house on their hands, the Burns finally realized that it was time to call in the experts.

In the summer of 1983, a team of paranormal investigators, led by the famous ghost hunter Norman Basile, met at the Old Homestead Road acreage. The team interviewed Rod and Angela about their experiences in the house, then toured the grounds. The ghost hunters noted with interest that there seemed to be evidence of a Native American burial mound not far from the house. The Burns family then left, and the investigative team settled in for an eventful night in the house.

Within hours, the group had amassed enough evidence to convince themselves that the house was filled with negative energy and spiritual activity. They experienced cold spots, repugnant odors and strong sensations of fear emanating from the crawl space beneath the home. All of the investigators agreed that there was a very malevolent presence in the spare bedroom, and when the woman of the group lay on the bed, it began to shake violently. Photos taken inside the house showed nothing unusual, but photos of the exterior all developed with strange streaks of light across them. The infrared film that was used that night was later developed to show the same slashes of light—as well as faces superimposed upon the house's windows.

Everyone felt that there was a strong, almost electrical energy in the building. In the pre-investigation interview, Rod had mentioned seeing strange lightning that seemed to be crawling across the ground, outside. Norman Basile claimed that he could even hear a crackling, popping sound of electricity. The ghost hunters agreed; the spirits did not want the Burns family there, and were summoning powerful negative forces to destroy them. Something had to be done.

The group decided on an appeasement ritual. The doors and windows of the house were opened wide, and each room was filled with candles, incense and special oils. Outside, the ghost hunters stood in a square formation. Each drove a metal rod into the ground and stood beside it. The atmosphere became charged with spiritual energy. Suddenly, Norman Basile could see a crowd of apparitions watching. Undaunted, Basile dug a hole in the center of the square, and filled it with salt and corn. As these gifts to the spirits were covered up with earth, one member of the group asked for a sign that a bargain had been struck. A sound pierced the air: it sounded like the excited whooping characteristic of Native American celebrations.

The ghostly activity decreased considerably after the appeasement ritual, but Rod and Angela Burns still felt it necessary to put their house up for sale. They were instructed by the ghost hunters to stay clear of the four stakes until they had moved out, and then to pull them out of the ground to release the spirits. They did as they were told.

The unassuming house on Old Homestead Road belongs to someone else now. It is unknown whether the resident spirits have kept up their part of the bargain, and remained quiet.

The Irish Castle

Among the lovely homes and manicured lawns in the Chicago neighborhood of Beverly sits a majestic, gray limestone castle. If you visit it on a Sunday, you may see crowds of people filing into it, because it is now the home of the Beverly Unitarian Church. But the friendly parishioners are not the only attraction: after 114 years of existence, it has also accumulated a number of charming ghosts.

It looks like something out of 14th-century Ireland, because it was originally built to satisfy an eccentric longing. The Irish Castle, as it is called, was constructed in 1886 for a developer named Robert Givens. Givens was building a home for his bride, and wanted what he considered to be the very best—a place reminiscent of the stately, centuries-old castles in his native Ireland. Some say the lady died before she lived in her new home; others claim that she simply disliked the ostentatious abode. For whichever reason, the Irish Castle was destined to be passed on to the ownership of others.

Prior to becoming a church, the mansion was home to a manufacturer, a doctor, the Chicago Female College and a girls' boarding school. The parade of tenants seems to have left a variety of psychic imprints on the castle; reported ghost sightings date back nearly 70 years.

One well-known story relates that influenza swept through the boarding school in the 1930s. One young girl named Clara died, and is still seen there to this day. Reverend Leonetta Bugleisi recalled meeting her on February 27, 1994, only minutes after being installed as pastor of the church. Bugleisi had turned to look at her husband, when she suddenly saw two willowy arms encircle the man's waist. Her husband did not feel the spectral hug, but both felt that it must have been a sign of welcome.

Another of the castle's gentle spirits is a woman who can sometimes be glimpsed in the garden. Many believe her to be the apparition of Eleanor Veil, who once lived in the castle and lovingly cared for its surrounding landscape.

Then, there are the miscellaneous phenomena for which there are no explanations or theories. They include the tinkling sounds of dinnerware; distant, disembodied voices; glimpses of candles passing by the windows when the building was known to be empty; and items that have mysteriously gone missing. The misty figure of a woman in a flowing white nightdress is seen wandering the property on occasion. And one New Year's Eve, a very real-looking lady in red descended the stairs and moved toward a door, which opened magically before her. She then walked away across a pristine blanket of snow, leaving no trail of footprints.

If ever you're looking for a haunt where the ghosts are friendly and the atmosphere medieval, visit Chicago's only castle. It is guaranteed not to disappoint.

A Shared Spirit

Gertrude and Russell Meyers were newlyweds in the summer of 1935 when they rented a modest bungalow in the suburbs of Bloomington. She was a high school teacher; he worked nights as a stereotyper at the local newspaper. Because of their conflicting schedules, each of the Meyers spent a great deal of time alone in their new home. Or so they thought.

It was late autumn when Gertrude began to suspect that she was not entirely alone. As the evenings grew increasingly cooler, and closed windows muffled the noise of traffic, the sounds from within the house became more obvious. On more than one occasion, Gertrude had the impression that someone or something was walking from room to room with her, but she would shrug the feeling off, convincing herself that it was only her lively imagination.

One evening, Gertrude retired early and, in contrast to her usual practice, left the bedroom door ajar. At approximately 10:30, just as she was about to fall asleep, she heard quick, heavy footsteps moving through the house. The sound started by the front door, moved through the living room and dining room, and then started down the hall toward the bedroom. Terrified, Gertrude leaped from under the covers and slammed the door. She slid the lock shut and waited, her heart pounding, to see what the intruder would do.

Nothing happened. Gertrude waited for what seemed an eternity, but no one attempted to break down the bedroom door. Nor was there a sound of retreating footsteps. Eventually, she was able to convince herself that she had been dreaming, or that the sounds had actually come from the street. She fell asleep, and in the morning chose not to tell her husband about her foolishness.

As time went on, Gertrude Meyers began to realize that the footsteps, although inexplicable, were real enough. Night after night at 10:30, she heard the familiar pattern of someone stomping from the front door to the bedroom. One evening, Gertrude summoned the courage to throw open the bedroom door just as the footsteps stopped on the other side—but she was greeted by nothing more than an empty hall.

The invisible guest continued to pay his nightly visits, and Gertrude continued to keep them a secret. She didn't want Russell thinking that his sensible, educated wife was prone to hallucinations, nor did she want him wondering if they were beginning their married life in a haunted house. What she didn't know was that Russell was having strange experiences of his own.

During the day, while Gertrude was at work and Russell was at home, his sleep was often interrupted by the sound of footsteps. When he got up to investigate, he always found himself alone. Even more mysterious was that, when he arrived home from work at 3:30 AM and went down to the basement to stoke the furnace, he could hear his wife wandering about on the main floor. But when he went upstairs to greet her, she would always be back in bed, soundly sleeping.

One night Russell confronted Gertrude about her nocturnal ramblings. Her response convinced him that the footsteps he had been hearing were not hers. His question convinced her that she was not the only one aware of their home's strange sounds. Finally, the two began to compare experiences, and realized that they could no longer dismiss the incredible: their house had a ghost.

There was a certain comfort in having shared their fears. Besides, the ghost seemed harmless enough. The winter wore on, the footsteps continued, and the young couple learned to accept the noise as a feature of the old house.

Spring finally arrived. As the ice melted and the ground thawed, Gertrude and Russell began exploring the backyard. They hadn't had time to tend it in the fall, and since then it had been buried in snow. Only after the snow had disappeared did they discover a small garden plot. The thought of fresh vegetables was appealing, so they decided to do some planting. One warm afternoon in May, while they were outdoors opening seed packets and working with hoes, they finally met their neighbors.

An elderly woman and her 25-year-old grandson lived in the house next door. As the Meyers spoke with them, they discovered that the layout of their home was a mirror image of the neighbors'. And, as the conversation continued, they began to suspect that they shared more than a similar floor plan.

The neighbors confided that they had a spirit in their home—one that stomped about in heavy footwear, often around 10:30 at night.

But how could identical houses have identical ghosts?

Gertrude and Russell Meyers eventually discovered that their home and the neighbors' home had once been a single structure, a duplex of sorts. The building had been separated into two free-standing houses and then rented out. The previous owner had lived on the premises—and had died there by his own hand. The footsteps heard in both homes were likely his. The man's ghost was either unaware that his home had been divided in two, or else felt entitled to haunt both halves.

The Persistent Presence

In July 1997, a woman named Sue Hieber wrote to *FATE* magazine about a strange experience she'd had more than 30 years before.

"When my husband and I moved into an old house in Peoria, Illinois, in 1965," Hieber wrote, "we noticed a cold draft in the bedroom." She and her husband followed the chill into the bedroom's walk-in closet, and found that, there in the ceiling, a hatchway to the attic had been left uncovered. Hieber's husband climbed onto a precarious pile of furniture in order to reach the opening, and managed to pull the heavy hatch cover securely into place.

But the draft came back. The next morning, Hieber and her husband awoke to the same chilled air, and traced it to the same source: the open attic hatchway. Hieber's husband blamed the dislodging of the cover on the vibrations of a passing train, but Hieber herself suspected a more supernatural cause.

"I kept telling my husband that I felt a 'presence' in the room that just did not want the attic shut off," she explained. "I felt the presence would not harm us if my husband left it alone."

Hieber's husband wasn't willing to believe in ghosts or resign himself to sleeping in a frigid room. After five nights of replacing the 30-pound door only to awaken to the draft again, he decided upon what he felt would be a final solution. He went into the closet one evening, pulled the cover over the opening, and then drove a number of long, sturdy, 20-penny nails through each of the four sides. Hieber told *FATE* that his comment to her was "Well, let's see your spook open that."

Of course, it did.

The next morning, the Hiebers awoke to the familiar draft—and something even more dramatic. The heavy wooden cover, which had been so tightly nailed down, had been ripped from its place and thrown 20 feet or more, into the farthest corner of the attic. The nails had not been removed first, but rather had been ripped through the wood laterally and so quietly that the two people who slept only a few feet away never heard a thing.

Hieber's skeptical husband never admitted to changing his mind about the possibility of ghosts, but did announce that day that he was unable to live in such a "drafty" house. They moved immediately thereafter.

Ghostly Gold

The abandoned Victorian house was 64 years old, boarded up, forgotten. It was slated for demolition because of a new road that the city planned to have run through the weed-choked lot. Sylvan and Francis, two curious teenaged boys, felt that one last look around the old place was in order. The date was March 23, 1955, and the adventure the boys experienced that day would never be forgotten.

They had been in the house only a few minutes when they heard a mysterious sound above them. The distant creaking of dry floorboards from one of the upper stories told Sylvan and Francis that they were not alone. Their instincts likely advised them to run, but each wanted to impress the other with his bravery. They started up the narrow staircase, and followed the sounds to the third floor.

What the two saw there annihilated their bravado and raised goose flesh on their arms. It was a tall man, well dressed in a silk top hat and an old-fashioned black coat. His somber expression unnerved the boys, but what shook them to the core was the fact that he was somewhat transparent. As Sylvan and Francis stood there, mouths gaping, looking at him and through him, the man raised one black-clad arm and beckoned.

The ghost glided slowly away across the old floor, and the boards creaked eerily as it passed over them. When it reached the farthest corner of the room, the specter slowly raised its arm once more, and pointed at a piece of ornate molding above one of the dormer windows. Then the apparition vanished into the dusty air.

The boys could hardly believe what they had witnessed, but were not too frightened to wonder about the meaning of the spirit's gesture. Cautiously, they crossed the room and began to

Abandoned houses almost always appear to be haunted. In 1955, two Illinois teens found one that was.

investigate the spot above the window. Sylvan discovered that knocking on the molding produced a hollow sound, so he pulled out a penknife and carefully pried the piece of wood away from the wall. Behind the molding, there was indeed a small cubbyhole and, within that, a leather pouch with a drawstring. The boys' hearts were pounding with anticipation as they pulled the pouch from its home and loosened the string. Sylvan tipped the bag toward his palm and held his breath.

Out poured a shining stream of coins. The late-afternoon sun coming through the dormer window gleamed warmly on the metal. Francis, who collected coins, recognized immediately that they were genuine, and that they were gold.

The pouch contained 18 rare gold coins, later appraised to be worth a total of $660. It would have been a shame had the money been lost under the tracks of a bulldozer.

Years later, Sylvan and Francis looked into the history of the old house where they had had the unbelievable adventure. In a newspaper dated March 23, 1905—exactly 50 years before the day of their discovery—they came across the obituary of Leonardus P. Elbert, the man who had built the house. There was a photo, and although several years had passed, Sylvan and Francis instantly recognized the face. Leonardus P. Elbert was the apparition they had faced that day, one-half century after his death, and only days before his beloved home was to be demolished.

Had Elbert haunted the house for 50 full years, or simply shown up on the anniversary of his death for one last look around? The only thing that's certain is this: for Sylvan and Francis, the little pouch filled with gold was truly a gift from beyond the grave.

Chapter 7

TALES FROM ADAMS COUNTY

Harry Middleton Hyatt, a professor at Culver-Stockton College in Canton, Missouri, devoted much of his lifetime to collecting stories from the people who lived across the Mississippi River from where he taught. The result of his efforts was the 1935 book Folk-Lore From Adams County Illinois. *It contains a number of compelling ghostly yarns, filled with fascinating details that depict life in Adams County in the late 19th and early 20th centuries.*

Here is a handful of engaging stories, based upon the original tales collected by Professor Hyatt.

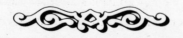

A Phantom in the Fire

There was once a saloon on South Fifth Street in Quincy that was operated by a husband and his wife. It was a pleasant place to stop for a drink, and before long the couple had a strong business with a number of regular customers. Unbeknownst to their clientele, they also had a ghost: the pale but well-defined apparition of a woman wandered the corridor in the living quarters upstairs. Perhaps they questioned their own senses. Perhaps they were afraid they would be ridiculed. The worst possibility was that the ghost would drive away business. For whatever reason, the saloonkeeper and his wife never said a word about their spectral boarder. The spirit upstairs did not meddle with the spirits downstairs, and all was well.

One night there was a terrible fire. The flames quickly consumed the old wooden building, and the couple and their children, clinging to a few belongings, barely escaped with their lives. Once safely across the street, they joined the crowd and watched with sadness as their home and their business were destroyed. Orange flames licked wildly at the night sky as the shingles ignited. Only seconds before the roof collapsed, the saloonkeeper's wife saw a figure in one of the upstairs windows. It was the ghost, gazing sadly down at the crowd below.

One year later, the family had recovered from its loss. The husband and wife had established another saloon in the same neighborhood, and were enjoying great success. The old customers had followed them, and several new ones had discovered them. Business was good and the future looked bright.

Quincy, Adams County.

One day, an out-of-town client who had not been seen since the evening of the fire came into the saloon. As he tipped his glass, he offered his belated condolences to the proprietor, stating that it had indeed been a tragedy. The saloonkeeper shrugged it off, insisting that the new business was doing well. The fire had really been no more than an inconvenience.

"But your wife!" the man exclaimed. "You lost your wife in the fire!"

The saloonkeeper quickly assured his customer that his wife was alive and well. In fact, she was resting upstairs at that very moment. "No one was harmed in that fire," he said.

"But I swear to you," the man insisted, "that with my own two eyes I saw the roof fall in upon a woman who was standing at an upper window! Who was that woman?"

The saloonkeeper did not answer, but from that point on, he and his wife knew that their ghostly guest had not simply been a figment of their imaginations.

John's Reward

In the mid-1800s, a cholera epidemic swept through Adams County. The terrible disease devastated the community, attacking young and old alike. Entire families were taken ill, leaving no one healthy enough to care for the sick. It was a time when people learned to count on their neighbors. One man in particular was known to always be there to help. He was a pious Irish fellow named John, and was a kind friend to anyone who needed him. During the epidemic, John tirelessly nursed and comforted those who were ill, and diligently buried those who had succumbed. He believed that no one should be alone in their time of need.

Given the highly infectious nature of the disease, John's contracting it was inevitable. He was the last person in the community to get sick. Home alone with his wife, he began to feel the violent effects of the illness. Darkness had fallen, and no one knew that John was ailing. His wife was faced with a terrible decision. It was clear to the woman that her husband would not live through the night, and she dared not leave his side. But there was no one else who could go to fetch the priest, and John, a devout Catholic, needed his last rites.

As the poor woman anxiously considered her choices, there was a knock at the door. When she answered it, she could not believe her eyes. There stood the parish priest.

"I have been called to come to John," he said solemnly. The priest was unsure who had given him the message, as was John's wife, since she was the only one who had known that he had taken ill.

John died that night, but not without the sacramental rites. In his lifetime, he always helped others in their time of need. When his time came, John received help, too—perhaps from above, perhaps from some grateful soul from beyond the grave.

The Haunted Cabin

Many years ago, a young couple was traveling with their infant child, searching for a place to settle and a way to make a living. They were growing tired and desperate when they came upon an abandoned log house near Kingston, Illinois. The place was filthy from years of disuse, but was sturdy enough in structure. "Let's camp here," said the husband. "You make some lunch, and I'll go find water for the horses." He wandered off in search of a spring, leaving his wife to unpack their few provisions.

Minutes later, there was a bloodcurdling scream. With his heart racing, the young man ran back toward the cabin, and found his wife in the yard, clutching their crying child. Before he could even ask, she was telling him, "This house is haunted! We had been inside only a minute when an old man with a cane appeared! He walked around us and then went out the door!"

The husband soothed her as best he could. "You just imagined it," he insisted. "We're all tired, and will feel better once we've had a bite to eat." Eventually, the woman calmed down enough to prepare a meal, which the weary young family ate in silence.

After lunch, the husband announced that he was going to walk up the road to a distant farm house he had spotted. "I might be able to find some work there," he said hopefully, and set off.

The farmer who owned the neighboring land appeared bemused when the young man told him that he was looking for work and permission to stay in the cabin. "I could use some help," said the farmer, "but there's no one who's stayed in that cabin more than one night." When the young fellow assured him that he could not be frightened off by spooks, the farmer laughed. "Tomorrow morning, if you still want to stay, come on over here and I'll put you to work."

While the husband was out talking to the farmer, his wife was visited once more by the apparition of the old man. This time, as the grizzled specter circled the terrified woman, he pointed his cane at her. She began to wail with fear, which prompted the old man to speak. "Do not be afraid," he rasped. "I will not harm you." The spirit then walked out the door, leaving the trembling woman to her chores.

The husband returned to the cabin, eager to share his good news about having found some work. When his wife greeted him with another hysterical ghost story, he was slightly irritated, and determined not to have their good fortune spoiled. "You are only seeing things," he assured her, and stubbornly refused to leave. As he relayed the afternoon's events, however, he deliberately omitted the farmer's warning about the cabin.

That night was uneventful, and early the next morning, the husband went off to his new job. A short time after he left, as the wife began to clear their few breakfast dishes, the ghost appeared for the third time. Again, the wizened specter walked around the room, pointing his cane at the woman. Again, she began to scream.

"Lady, I will not hurt you," the ghost repeated. "I have come to do you good. My wife and I were murdered here for our money—only, the robbers did not get it. I want you and your husband to do something for me. We are buried out here in a cave. I want you to take us up and bury us on the hill in the graveyard and mark the place."

In exchange for a proper burial, the ghost showed the woman where two stashes of money were buried. He marked one spot on the dirt floor of the cellar, and another on the ground by the southeast corner of the house. "Down here, you'll find a box of money and the deed to this little house," he explained. "Do what I ask of you, and the place is yours." The old man then pointed out the nearby cave where the couple would find the skeletal remains. "That is where we are buried," he said sadly, and disappeared.

The young woman's fear had been replaced with overwhelming curiosity. As soon as the ghost had vanished, she hurried down into the cellar to dig in the spot he had marked. She had scooped away only a few handfuls of the dry, dirt floor when she was rewarded. There, buried inches below the surface, was an ancient, chipped pitcher—filled to the brim with money.

When her husband walked through the door that evening, the wife could not contain her news. "I have made more money than you, today!" she exclaimed. The man didn't know what to make of her outburst, but could see that something was amiss, because the breakfast dishes still sat out and the cleaning had not been started. Still, he listened patiently as his wife told her fantastic story. When she showed him the jug of coins—more money than the young couple had ever had at one time—his jaw dropped. "Remember, there's more outside," the wife reminded him. "We are also to dig by the corner of the house."

The man picked up his battered shovel and followed his wife to the spot that had been marked. As promised, there was a metal box, stuffed with more cash and the deed to the cabin. The ghost had not exaggerated.

The very next morning, the young couple lived up to their part of the strange bargain. They walked up to the cave, found the remains of the old man and his wife, and placed them in a nice, pine coffin. In the cemetery, near the top of the hill, they said some respectful words and put the pine box in a proper grave. Then they filled in the grave and marked it with a modest, but dignified, headstone. The house and money were now theirs—and the ghost, who must have agreed, never appeared to them again.

"Pray for Me"

There was once a young couple in Adams County who had been dating for many months. The girl expected that her boyfriend would someday ask her to be his wife, but during one particularly bitter argument, the young man spat out, "I will never marry you!" The girl was devastated, and worried about it so much that she finally took her own life.

The rather callous boyfriend had a new girl on his arm in no time. It wasn't long, however, before his carefree life was interrupted by the ghost of his dead girlfriend. Every time the fellow tried to walk to his new girl's house, he would be confronted on the street by his ex-lover's mournful spirit. She would say nothing, but neither would she let him pass. Eventually, the young man would give up, go home, and worry about the situation. When it got to the point where he could not eat or sleep, he decided to consult a priest.

The kindly priest listened to the distraught fellow's strange story, and offered a suggestion. "Tonight, when you see the spirit," he said, "call to her by name. Then ask, 'What is wrong that you can't rest in your grave?'"

Armed with this advice, the young man set out on his evening walk. Before long, he saw her: the pale, sad apparition of his former girlfriend hovered before him on the street. As she blocked his path with her misty form, he asked her the question. The ghost parted her lips, and, appearing to summon all her strength, wailed the words, "Pray for me, pray for me." She then vanished in a burst of cold, white light—leaving her boyfriend more confused than ever.

The man did as the spirit asked. He went directly home and prayed for the girl's soul all through the night. At dawn, he returned to the church and spoke once more with the priest. The priest listened to the story and told the man, "I will hold a special mass and try to understand why that poor soul wants us to pray. Until then, you continue to pray for her every single hour."

The next day at 5 AM, the priest held a mass and prayed for understanding. His concentration was such that he became soaked in perspiration, and oblivious to his surroundings. Eventually, however, he was granted insight into the dead girl's anguish. Later that day, he called the young man.

"You had a very serious relationship with this woman," he said. "Perhaps you were considering marriage." The young fellow nodded, although he was a bit surprised. He had been deliberately vague when telling the priest about his history with the girl.

"I believe she ended her life because she felt you had forsaken her—but that is not why she cannot rest. There was another, dire consequence of your failed romance."

The young man leaned forward, eager to hear the priest explain.

"She was carrying your child," the older man finally said. "She is tortured because, when she killed herself, she also killed your unborn baby."

The boyfriend was shocked. For the first time in his life, perhaps, he felt a sense of responsibility. His cold-hearted actions had caused an enormous amount of pain. Seeing this, he resolved immediately to make things right. He prayed for forgiveness and for the peace of his girlfriend's soul, and made every effort to change his heartless ways with women. His reformation must have been effective, because eventually the sorrowful spirit found rest and no longer stopped him on the street.

Spirits in Crisis

One of the most common kind of ghost is the so-called "crisis apparition." Crisis apparitions are spirits that appear to loved ones at a time of trouble, often to communicate emergency or death. Stories of these ominous visits have been collected from around the world, and Illinois is no exception. The following four tales hail from Adams County.

* * *

"When I was nine years old," one man said, "my father was quite sick. One cool evening at dusk, I went to the spring to get a bucket of water."

The boy was on his way back to the house when he met his father on the path. The youngster thought that his dad was feeling better, and had come to help him with the heavy pail, so he reached forward to offer him the handle. The father did not take it, however, nor did he look at his boy. Instead, he strode right past him and continued down the path. The boy watched him for a few moments, until he realized that his father was walking toward the nearby cemetery. Feeling uncomfortable and suddenly very eager for the warmth of his mother's kitchen, the boy hurried home.

When he arrived, his mother noticed how pale and shaken her son appeared. She asked him what was wrong, and the lad said, "I just met father down the path."

"Then that was his spirit you saw," the mother said. "For he has not been out of his room."

"Later that week," concluded the man, "my father died of his illness." He was buried in the cemetery at the end of the path.

* * *

There was a little girl whose mother worked for a woman named Miss Nancy. One morning, as the girl was walking along the path by the cemetery, she met Miss Nancy.

"She was all dressed up," the girl later told her mother, "Wearing her new sunbonnet, and walking straight into the cemetery." The girl's mother shook her head sadly.

"You only met her spirit, for Miss Nancy is very sick and cannot get out of bed."

Sadly, it was true. Within a few days, Miss Nancy was dead.

* * *

Generations ago, a man named Johnson was driving his wagon down a quiet country road toward his home. Dusk was falling. Suddenly, Johnson's horse shied. The man stopped his wagon and calmed the animal, then looked up the road to see what it was that had frightened it so.

Johnson was both pleased and surprised to see his brother standing in the middle of the road. The brother lived some distance away, and it was unlike him to visit unannounced, but Johnson was happy to see him. He called out his brother's name, and began walking up the dirt road to greet him. Then, abruptly and silently, the man vanished. Confused, Johnson froze. Far off, a lone sparrow chirped softly. Eventually Johnson climbed back into the driver's seat and continued on home.

Several hours later, Johnson learned that his brother had passed away—at exactly the time he met the ghostly image in the road.

* * *

A young woman was once forced to undergo emergency surgery in a hospital in Chicago. Her family, who lived in Quincy, knew nothing of the situation. The delicate operation began to go very badly, but those who loved her remained many miles away and quite unaware.

That night, the woman's mother awoke from a deep sleep, and was shocked to see her daughter's ghost standing beside the bed, weeping.

The next morning, as the family gathered at the breakfast table, the mother told them of the previous night's experience. "I'm certain your sister has died," she cried. "I saw her ghost so clearly."

The other family members were equally distraught. They all had great faith in their mother's visions. They even began to pack their bags for a trip to Chicago, believing that they would soon be called to attend their sister's funeral.

Later that day, a telegram arrived. The mother opened it with dread, preparing for the inevitable news. As she read it, however, she was overcome with relief. The cable told her of her daughter's operation, and that she had been very close to death. Just moments after the woman's spirit had appeared to her mother, though, the doctors had been able to save her life. She was expected to recover.

The family rejoiced, and looked forward to seeing their beloved sister and daughter in the flesh, to tell her of the moment she traveled to their home in spirit only.

The Ghost's Bedroom

A woman once rented a house that came with strange instructions from the landlord.

"We have always been friends," said the man, "so I will let you have this house. But I want you to promise one thing: lock my dead wife's bedroom, and never go into it. She told me before she died that she didn't want anyone to use it."

There was another bedroom in the house, and the woman lived alone, so she made the promise easily. The door was locked, and that room was never used.

Some time later, however, the woman's teenaged son lost his job and returned to live with his mother. He spent a few nights sleeping on an uncomfortable sofa in the living room, then began to press his mother about the locked bedroom.

"I am not afraid of ghosts," the boy insisted. "I'm going to take that for my room."

"Well," answered his mother, weary of the fight, "if you come out of that room screaming, don't blame me." She gave her son the key and he moved his belongings into the room that very day.

By the time the boy went to bed that evening, his bravado had diminished somewhat. Although it was a moonlit night, he left the lamp burning, certain that the light would comfort him. Before he had even closed his eyes, however, he was startled by a small white dog that materialized on the window sill.

"The dog jumped down on the floor," the boy reported later, "and when it jumped, it shook the whole house. It even scared my mother, for she screamed, 'What's wrong?'" The lad was so transfixed by the strange animal that he did not answer.

The lamp suddenly blew out, and the boy hurriedly relighted it. When light spilled across the room once more, the white dog was nowhere to be seen. In its place, at the foot of the boy's bed, stood the ghost of the landlord's departed wife. Her arms were folded and her features were twisted in anger.

The boy found the courage to speak. "What, in the name of the Father, Son and Holy Ghost, do you want?" he commanded, knowing full well what she would say. The specter told him, in no uncertain terms, that she did not want anyone staying in her private room. The young fellow appeared to consider this, then told her, "But I have no place to sleep. Can I not stay here?" To his delight, the entity appeared somewhat sympathetic, and proposed a compromise.

"If you will let no one come in the room but you—don't even let anyone sit down or change his clothes or do anything in this room—I will not bother you. But if you do let anyone in this room, beware!" On that dramatic note, the spirit disappeared.

A deal had been struck, and it was kept. The boy never let another person enter his bedroom, and the ghost never bothered him again.

Chapter 8

PUBLIC PHANTOMS

*If you prefer that your ghost
stories withstand rigorous scrutiny,
you'll be drawn to the public phantoms.
Because spirits in public places are often
experienced by large numbers of
independent witnesses, the stories are
much more objective and convincing.*

*For those who like to play the
amateur ghost hunter, these specters
also offer the added appeal of availability.
Their homes—restaurants, theaters, schools
and stores—are open to the public.
For the price of a meal or a show,
one has every right to sit in comfort
in the ghost's haunt, and wait for
something paranormal to occur.*

*Settle in with the following stories,
and plan your tour of haunted Illinois.*

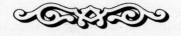

The Phantom of the Woodstock Opera

It is evening. Eva Bornstein, the executive director of the Woodstock Opera House, is leaving work for the day. She passes from her office through the empty theater, and a spring-loaded seat, which, strangely, has been in the lowered position, pops up. Bornstein continues on her way through the building, oblivious to the fact that a lobby door has opened and closed of its own volition. The woman's dog, who accompanies her, is more perceptive; the animal glances curiously over its shoulder at some unseen display.

Outside the picturesque theater, Bornstein slides behind the wheel of her shiny new car and drives away. It is then that the disembodied voice states, "She believes in Hondas, not ghosts."

This television commercial was aired by Honda during the 1992 Super Bowl. It featured the Woodstock Opera House, the theater's executive director at that time, and a ghost that is as famous as many of the great names that have graced the theater's stage. However, in terms of the limelight, this spirit is not greedy. Her legendary presence has easily garnered as much publicity for the playhouse as it has for her.

The Woodstock Opera House opened in the late 1800s, in the pretty little community of Woodstock in northern Illinois. Today, the four-story theater with its beautiful bell tower remains the tallest structure in the town, which is known for its historic homes and early 20th-century square. Fine architecture is not the only thing that has distinguished the opera house, however. Numerous actors who then went on to Hollywood fame have trodden upon its stage: Paul Newman, Shelley Berman, Tom Bosley, Geraldine Page, Betsy Palmer and Orson Welles are among the stars who once played there. In 1947, Berman was one of a group of young artists working diligently on a summer stock production. Many years later, he would tell of the strange experiences he had then.

Berman recalled rehearsing his dialogue in the theater late one night. As he finished his lines, he looked out across the empty auditorium and saw a single seat—DD113—pop up, as if some unseen guest had just exited. The sight was unsettling, and became more so each time it recurred over several evenings. During some rehearsals, Berman would see two seats next to each other lower at the same time. On one particularly memorable night, five seats went down at once.

When Berman began discreetly to share his stories, he found that other actors had been hearing mysterious footsteps and whispering voices. "When it had happened enough, we began to talk about it," Berman told *Rockford Magazine* in the fall of 1996. "We knew there was something in that place. It creaked too much, and you never felt you were alone. But the word 'ghost' was used very sparingly."

Over the years, however, the word "ghost" has been bandied about a great deal in association with the Woodstock Opera House. The spirit has even been given a name: she is called "Elvira." Some maintain that she was named after the apparition in Noel Coward's play *Blithe Spirit*; others, after the campy horror-movie mistress of the same name. Year after year and decade after decade, Elvira has performed her theatrical antics at the Woodstock Opera House.

When she wants to sit down, she invariably chooses her favorite spring-loaded seat, DD113. When a performance or rehearsal displeases her, the actors will often hear a deep sigh of disappointment coming from that seat. And if props shift around inexplicably, everyone knows who to blame.

Generally, Elvira is known for harmless disturbances, but there are those who say she has a darker side. They warn actresses who play leading roles at the Woodstock Opera House to stay clear of the bell tower. Some leading ladies, while surveying the view from high above the lovely town, have been overcome by a horrendous compulsion to jump. Rumor has it that the women were mesmerized by Elvira, and that Elvira is the ghost of a despondent actress who met her own death when she jumped from the tower nearly one century ago.

This rumor, according to the theater's management, is absolutely false. According to recent research about the opera house, no newspaper articles or minutes from town meetings make reference to such a suicide. And that era, as one manager put it, was a time when even "a person's trip to Chicago or a five-year-old's birthday party were covered in excruciating detail."

The management also dismisses the idea that there is anything paranormal happening in their place of business. But although they deny the existence of the ghost, they do not deny that she has had quite a beneficial effect on the theater's popularity. Manager Jan Link calls the ghost story "folklore," adding, "But it has worked wonders for the fame of the opera house."

The management has not always maintained such an aloof position with respect to Elvira. Several years ago, one executive director of the opera house not only admitted to the eerie phenomena caused by the ghost, but went so far as to describe them as "very unnerving." Once, a woman who served on the board of directors reported the rare experience of actually seeing Elvira. She described her as being very attractive, with long, golden hair and a flattering, flowing gown.

Today, some believe in the phantom of the opera house, and

some do not. Even Shelley Berman, who is certain that he encountered the ghost back in 1947, admits that, over the years, exaggeration has taken hold. "I think the story has grown a bit fat," Berman was quoted as saying in *Rockford Magazine.* He went on to say that it "has become old and hack... the kind that can be read in any dime magazine." Reading about a ghost pales in comparison to visiting its haunt oneself. If you ever get it in your mind to prove or disprove the existence of Elvira, attend a performance at the famous Woodstock Opera House, and keep a keep an eye peeled for activity in seat DD113. Who knows? You might see some entertainment that is not on the program.

The Country House Restaurant

One Sunday afternoon in 1957, a young blonde woman walked into the Country House Restaurant in Clarendon Hills. She had her child with her, and asked the bartender, with whom she was friendly, if she could leave the toddler for an hour while she ran an errand. The request was refused, and the blonde left the restaurant upset. Just a short distance down the road, the woman deliberately drove her car into a tree. Her child was unhurt, but the woman was killed.

This story was presented by a psychic named Evelyn Taglini as a conclusion to her investigation of the Country House Restaurant, which lies just west of Chicago. The owner had requested her help in explaining some strange phenomena that had been occurring at the popular restaurant for some time.

Taglini's discovery was terrible, almost unbelievable. But when the story found its way to the former owner of the restaurant, Richard Montanelli, he corrected only one detail: "It was 1958," he said. Montanelli knew, for he had been there.

No one is sure why the young mother committed suicide, but her spirit has since occupied the restaurant, which is renowned for its half-pound burgers and rustic atmosphere. From the day that the current owners, David and Patrick Regnery, bought the eatery in 1974, they knew that something was amiss.

Doors, windows and shutters would all open and close on their own. Staff members would report hearing voices, and customers waiting for a table would claim that the hostess had called their names when in fact she had not. Often someone would report a frigid column of air moving through the cozy restaurant, and late at night, after closing time, the few remaining staff would be startled when the jukebox began to play on its own.

Then there were the footsteps, which were often heard on the stairs when no one was there. David Regnery once offered his second-floor storage room to a friend who needed a temporary place to stay. The man was a police officer. Several nights, the officer was awakened by the sound of someone coming up the staircase. Each time, he scrambled for his flashlight and firearm. Eventually the fellow accepted that the "intruder" was of the spectral variety, and simply rolled over and went back to sleep.

Author Dylan Clearfield visited that same storage area some years later, and was not so indifferent. He reported being "psychically choked" while in the room, and felt "intense oppression" on the stairs leading to it. Although the ghost of the Country House Restaurant is believed to be harmless, encountering it is still very unnerving. Regnery once said that a certain member of his nighttime cleaning crew refused to work alone after spending one entire shift listening to the ghost sobbing.

The ghost of the woman has also been seen. Sometimes she hangs around the women's rest room, and once she beckoned a customer from an upstairs window. According to author Arthur Myers in *The Ghostly Register*, the customer walked in and joked, "What are you guys running here, a bordello?" Regnery immediately checked out the second floor, but found no one there.

Psychics who have visited the establishment more recently think that a second presence has now joined the young blonde woman. It is a churlish male, they say, who may be creating a sense of menace and discomfort.

As long as the food remains so good, however, and the wood fireplace is warmly lighted, it will take more than one or two ghosts to keep loyal customers away from the Country House Restaurant.

The Dedicated Librarian

In the 1984 movie *Ghostbusters*, one of the first specters encountered by the protagonists is in the New York Public Library. Employees of the Milner Library, at Illinois State University in Normal, likely watched the scene with a sense of déjà vu, for they have their own resident ghost. Her name is Ange.

When the university hired its first official librarian in 1890, it made a splendid choice. The woman's name was Angeline Vernon Milner, but she was known to all as "Ange." For 38 years, Ange Milner devoted herself to the university library. From the moment she took the position, it became her life. She worked there until the day she died in 1928.

Some time after Ange's death, the university built a new library, and named it in her honor. Milner Library was a fine facility, but it lacked a storage annex. As the building became overcrowded with new material, some of the older, lesser-used books were packed off to the third floor of Williams Hall, another campus building.

Whenever a member of the library staff would venture over to Williams Hall and unlock the storage room on the third floor to retrieve some requested item, he or she would have the strange feeling of not being alone. Walking among the stacks, staff would commonly feel inexplicable cold spots and the sensation of having "company." The presence would be so strong that some people reported actually stepping aside to allow whatever it was to pass. On some occasions, the spirit was even seen: a misty white apparition of a woman would walk up and down the aisles, examining the books. Most who have encountered her feel that she is the ghost of Ange Milner, and that she is haunting, not the hall, but the old books she loved so much. Judging from some of the stories, Ange still feels very responsible for those volumes.

The head research librarian and a clerk were once standing among Ange's books in Williams Hall, discussing moving some of them to a different location. Suddenly an invisible force began to push the books off the shelves, one by one. Ange's criticism was duly noted.

One phenomenon in particular suggests that the collection, rather than the hall, is haunted. Whenever any of the old books are removed from Williams Hall and brought back into the main circulation, strange things begin to happen at Milner Library as well.

110 years after she was hired, Ange Milner is still on the job.

The Red Lion Pub

On Chicago's North Side, the Red Lion Pub is a popular place to stop for a pint, a hearty English meal and a ghost story. Moreover, it is one of the city's most famous haunts, and features many ghostly entities that seem quite willing to perform for the patrons.

Psychics who have visited the place tend to agree that a number of spirits reside in the Red Lion. One is a rough-looking cowboy; another is a blonde man; a third takes the form of a dark, bearded man wearing a black hat. There is also a female presence whose identity is disputed. Some think her to be a flapper who was murdered in an upstairs apartment. Those who know the history of the building, however, insist that she is much more likely to be the ghost of a young, mentally handicapped woman named Sharon, who lived and died on the premises.

Whoever the female spirit is, she is known for wearing a bit too much lilac perfume and for occasionally playing nasty tricks on women who use the upstairs washroom. A waitress was once locked in there for nearly 20 minutes, unable to force her way out. The desperate woman was close to tears when the door suddenly swung open on its own.

The owner of the pub, John Cordwell, feels that another of the resident specters may be his own father. The elder Cordwell was a believer in the spirit world, and always promised his son that he would try to contact him from the other side. When John first bought the building, he renovated, and paid tribute to his dad with a beautiful stained-glass window accompanied by a brass plaque of dedication. Ever since, Cordwell claims to feel a great deal of spiritual energy emanating from the spot where the plaque hangs. Fortunately, it is positive energy. As Cordwell once told author Arthur Myers, "I think he was very pleased by it."

In fact, none of the ghosts who haunt the Red Lion Pub seem to be very menacing. Although some may have originally been tough characters from the building's unsavory past as a bookmaking joint, they appear to be harmless enough now. Most limit their activities to noisy footsteps, unexplained taps on the shoulder, and the calling out of people's names.

Conveniently, ghost hunters who crave something a little more dramatic need only walk across the street: the Red Lion Pub sits directly opposite the famed Biograph Theater, where John Dillinger ate his last tub of popcorn. (See "Dillinger's Last Show," p. 39) It's a rather comfortable arrangement: ghost enthusiasts can enjoy a drink and a bite to eat and then take in a movie, all while soaking up some of the most ghostly atmosphere on Chicago's North Side.

All Souls' Day
at St. Rita's

There was one autumn in Chicago in the early 1960s when the spirits waited until two days after Halloween to make an appearance. When they did, however, it was spectacular, and witnessed by no fewer than 15 astonished onlookers.

It was November 2, All Souls' Day on the Catholic calendar. Although there were no official services being held at St. Rita's Church that day, 15 parishioners had gathered in the pews to pray for the souls of the departed. The church was softly lighted by flickering candles. All was quiet, except for the occasional murmured prayer.

Then, for 60 seconds that seemed to last an eternity, the peace was broken.

The organ, which had been silent, suddenly let out an unearthly wail. The startled people looked up from the pews to see who the prankster was, and were shocked to find that no one sat at the keyboard. Still the wretched screeching continued, and someone noticed that the hands of the clock had begun to spin around furiously in opposite directions. As the cacophony went on, six apparitions materialized around the discordant instrument.

They appeared to be monks. Three were robed in white, and three in black. At the sight of them, the members of the small congregation found the energy to flee, but were blocked at the exits: the doors had been firmly locked by some unseen force. As the parishioners huddled, terrified, at the back of the church, the monks began to glide through the pews toward them. They moved swiftly, effortlessly, floating several inches above the floor. The

Spiritual activity is expected in a church, but parishioners experienced something completely unfamiliar on one historic day at St. Rita's.

sound from the organ climaxed in a final shriek. It was then the parishioners heard the voice. Ubiquitous and disembodied, it whispered, "Pray for us."

As the supernatural sounds faded away, the doors blew open, and the 15 shocked witnesses scrambled to escape. They ran without looking back.

The whole ordeal lasted less then 60 seconds. It is unlikely, however, that any one of the parishioners ever forgot the desperate imperative they heard whispered on that All Souls' Day in St. Rita's.

The Presence of Pemberton Hall

The year is 1916. The place, Eastern Illinois University, in Charleston. Pemberton Hall, the women's dormitory, is besieged by a nighttime thunderstorm. Across the deserted campus, the wind howls, and rain lashes mercilessly against the windows and doors. Inside "Pem Hall," where it is warm and dry, one sleepless student tiptoes quietly up to the fourth-floor music room. She doesn't want to disturb anyone, but if she can't sleep, she wants to practice piano. Amidst the violent sounds of the storm, she reasons, no one will hear her. No one will even know that she is there.

The girl is right on one account, but wrong on the other. No one will hear her above the raging elements. But someone does know she is there. She is being watched.

The soft notes of the piano can be heard only faintly on the stairway leading to the isolated music room. Up those stairs, a large, menacing figure advances. His heart beats madly; his eyes are wild and bright. This is what he has been waiting for: finally, he has caught one of them alone.

She screams once, but her voice is no match for the din of the storm.

When he leaves, he is certain she is dead. Within minutes, he will be right, but for now a dim consciousness, a faint will to struggle against the brutal horror, survives. Bruised and bloody, the girl somehow summons the strength to inch down the staircase and crawl along the quiet hall. Finally, she reaches the door of a trusted counselor named Mary Hawkins. Unable to lift her nearly lifeless form from the floor, she scratches pitifully on the wood. When Counselor Hawkins opens the door, it is a moment too late. The girl's battered body lies dead, in a dark and spreading pool of blood.

Mary Hawkins is overcome with guilt. Even after the body has been removed, even after the calamitous news has swept through the school and the town and died down again, a single, unflagging thought tortures her conscience day and night: a girl who was in her charge was killed. When she sleeps, her nightmares are dominated by the image of the slain girl and the knowledge that the door was answered too late. When she wakes, she is haunted by her memories. Finally, when she can cope no longer, Mary Hawkins takes her own life. But death offers no escape: more than 80 years later, Mary Hawkins' spirit remains doomed to walk the halls of the dormitory, doomed eternally to watch over "her girls".

This grisly story is not true, according to Doris Enochs, who spent 10 years as a Pemberton Hall counselor. A woman named Mary Hawkins did work as a dorm counselor from 1910 to 1917. The woman did die, and is honored with a commemorative plaque in the hall's lobby. But Enochs has dismissed the rest of the story as sheer fantasy, stating that there have never been any records of a murder in Pem Hall. The tale is merely a tradition: the upperclassmen use it annually to frighten the freshmen. And each time it is told, according to Enochs, it becomes a little more dramatic.

The fact that a few different versions of the story exist indicates that it may be more deeply rooted in folklore than in fact. Nevertheless, Pemberton Hall is the site of some very strange occurrences. Even the no-nonsense Doris Enochs has admitted that "some weird things happen there."

For many decades, residents of Pemberton Hall have reported experiencing some very unusual phenomena. Furniture has been known to move without assistance. Lights flash, and windows open inexplicably—even on the fourth floor, which has long been locked and off-limits. There are sometimes footsteps heard in the hallways, and light rapping sounds at the doors, but whenever anyone investigates, the hallways are empty. On some frightening occasions, there have been a few bloody footprints left behind. They are visible for a few minutes, and then vanish.

Occasionally, faint strains of piano music can be heard coming from the fourth floor. There is still a piano up there, but the floor has been securely closed off for years. On the stairs that now lead to nowhere, an even more unnerving noise is occasionally heard. Residents describe it as a sickening, dragging sound.

Though they attract less attention, some of the supernatural events at Pemberton Hall are quite the opposite of harmful. Doors that have been left unlocked are always secured by morning, and radios and televisions that have been left playing are dutifully shut off before their owners return. It does seem that there could be at least two ghosts haunting Pemberton Hall—one who acts the part of a counsellor, and one who might be reliving a violent end. Could it be?

Whether there is even a grain of truth to the murder story remains doubtful. Still, among the fresh-faced students who regularly come and go, there are some residents of a more permanent—if not eternal—nature residing within the gothic stone walls of haunted Pemberton Hall.

The Spooky Speakeasy

During the Prohibition years, thousands upon thousands of illegal drinking establishments sprang up in cities and towns across the United States. Decatur, Illinois was no exception. One of its most popular speakeasies was on the third floor of a building that still exists in the 100 block of East Prairie Street. Today, the ground floor of the historic building—it was built in 1865—houses Bell's Jewelry, while much of the notorious third story is empty. Or so it seems.

Unusual things began to happen there in 1994, when portions of the block were undergoing a renovation. One workman who was on the third floor spent the afternoon thinking he was listening to a party on the other side of the wall: he was constantly disturbed by laughter, loud talking, music and something that sounded like the spinning of a roulette wheel. Later, he discovered that on the other side of the wall was a locked, abandoned room. Nothing was there now—there was no sign of a roulette wheel—but long ago, he learned, the room had been used for illegal drinking and gambling.

A couple of years later, employees at the jewelry store became exasperated when items began to go missing. Many would turn up later, in some unusual location, while others were simply gone for good. Loud footsteps were often heard coming from the third floor, but when some brave person would investigate, the place was always found empty—and strangely cold. On one mysterious occasion, the employees came to work in the morning and found that every one of the jewelry cases had been unlocked sometime during the night. The culprit had managed to do it without tripping the alarm system. What's more, nothing had been stolen. Eventually, a paranormal investigator named Troy Taylor was brought in to gather impressions in and assess the former speakeasy.

Taylor brought along a ghost hunter and psychic named Frank Ward. Ward supposedly had no knowledge of the place's history, but as he toured the rooms, he immediately received impressions that they had been used for drinking, gambling and other illicit purposes. He related a number of other accurate details, then announced that he had made contact with a spirit named Flossie Martin. As Flossie named off a list of other ghosts that were present in the speakeasy, Troy Taylor jotted down the names. None of them were familiar to him, until he made a trip to the public library. There, Taylor examined the burial records and city directories, and was able to account for every name on Flossie's list. All had lived and died in Decatur during the time that the speakeasy was in operation.

Prohibition may be over, but there are still spirits aplenty stashed away in this one Decatur speakeasy.

Harriet Haskell's Haunt

Lewis and Clark Community College in Godfrey, Illinois, should be famous for the dedication shown by its staff. One woman, Ms. Harriet Newell Haskell, is still showing up for work—more than a century after she was hired.

Harriet Haskell was the most beloved headmistress of the college in its early years, when it was known as the Monticello Female Seminary. She was once described as "not only an educator, but a vital, uplifting force to the students, and also their tender, sympathetic friend." The "Haskell Girls," as they called themselves, loved Harriet, and she was equally attached to them. For 40 years, Harriet Haskell devoted herself to her college and her students. Some swear that her devotion did not end with her death.

Custodians at Lewis and Clark College have long complained that the elevators, lights and water fountains seem to operate as though they have minds of their own. Even the furniture has been known to move about without human assistance. Students have often reported meeting the spectral headmistress in the deserted and darkened hallways late at night. She is always clad in a long black skirt and a high-collared white blouse. Some female students have wakened in their dorm rooms to find Ms. Haskell standing at the foots of their beds. Others catch an eerie glimpse of her in their mirrors, then turn around to find that no one is there.

The library, where Haskell lay in state after her death, seems to be one of the ghost's favorite locations. The librarians have often shuddered at the sensation of having someone unseen watch them as they go about their duties. Some have even felt a cold, spectral hand on their shoulder. One student who was studying in the library looked up from her books to see the apparition of an older woman praying. Gradually, the image faded away, leaving the student shaken and unable to concentrate for the remainder of the evening.

Psychics agree that the college is haunted, and that the ghost is undoubtedly Harriet Haskell. One sensitive woman, when taken into a particular room in the college, immediately felt an unbearable pain on the left side of her face. She could not have known that, in that very room, Harriet's face had been badly burned. The headmistress had dressed up as Santa Claus for her students one Christmas, and her whiskers had caught fire.

Another psychic, from St. Louis, has been to the college several times. On her very first visit, she was lucky enough to meet Harriet. She described her as "a woman in a long black skirt wearing a white high-collared blouse with a pin at the neck. She had scars on one side of her face." The apparition faded away silently when the woman tried to approach her.

There can be no question that it was Harriet Haskell, still watching over the college that she loved.

A Happy-Hour Afterlife

Many years ago, on Chicago's far North Side, a man named Frank Giff discovered his own little version of heaven. More than anything, Frank loved to drink, so he opened a tavern, which allowed him unlimited access to his favorite poison. Phrases like "last call" and "closing time" never apply to the proprietor of a bar, and Frank exploited this fact to full advantage.

Frank Giff happily ran his establishment, and even more happily indulged in his nightly binges. It was quite common for him to drink until he had passed out either in one of the booths along the wall or with his head on the bar. One night in 1964, Frank's excess rendered him more than unconscious: he was found dead the next morning in one of his usual drunken positions.

Frank Giff's family sold his beloved bar, and the establishment underwent several changes in name and ownership. One thing remained constant, however: the ghost of Frank continued to imbibe and carry on, as though he were oblivious to his death.

Shot glasses have been known to fly off the shelves, as though some unseen tippler was trying to set up another round. Women—particularly redheads—often feel a cool, invisible hand stroking their legs. What the current owners of the bar find most annoying is that the spirit continues to help himself to the other spirits behind the bar. No matter how securely the booze is locked up at night, there always seems to be less of it, come morning.

Apparently, as long as his former establishment is operating as a nightspot, death will be one endless party for the rowdy barkeep named Frank Giff.

The Ghosts of Millikin University

College students do love to have a resident spook to talk about. Students attending Millikin University in Decatur are luckier than most: they have several. In fact, it might be difficult to find a building on campus that isn't haunted. This university, which will soon celebrate its 100th birthday, may hold the distinction of being the most haunted school in all of Illinois.

If ever you tour Millikin University with the hope of studying something spectral, make sure to visit the following locations.

Albert Taylor Theater

Is it superstition or merely tradition? Different people will give you different answers about the ritual at the Albert Taylor Theater: before every performance, actors make sure to leave out three pieces of candy. If they don't, the ghost of the theater—a mischievous little girl—will supposedly ruin the show. She has been known to tamper with lights, sets, sound equipment and even the actors themselves.

Most performers leave the candy out of deference to the custom of the theater, but at least one woman does so out of unshakable belief in the ghost's existence. The actress had originally scoffed at the legend and refused to leave the traditional offering. Later that evening, she was walking down a flight of stairs prior to making her entrance on stage, when suddenly she felt two hands grab hold of her ankles. The woman regained her balance, then looked down, but could see nothing there. Still, she could feel the fingers tightening their hold. She tried to struggle free, but the invisible hands would not loosen their grip. Then the woman's feet were pulled out from under her, and she tumbled to the bottom of the stairs. She lay unconscious for some time. The actress missed that evening's performance, and never neglected to leave candy for the ghost again.

The Old Gymnasium

The old gymnasium at Millikin University was built in 1911, eight years after the institution opened. Eventually, a new facility was constructed—the Griswold Physical Education Center—and the original gym was rarely used, at least by the living.

One feature in the old gym was an elevated running track. Today, that track is used as a storage area by the drama department. It is always jammed full of props and sets. The fact that the track is completely blocked has done nothing to stop one spectral jogger, however. He has been heard making the circuit, his feet pounding out a steady rhythm as he runs one lap after another.

Another less physically active spirit can sometimes be heard weeping downstairs. The mournful sound eludes exact pinpointing. The woman's crying will grow louder and more anguished until the investigating person is sure she must be very near. Then it will stop, as though someone has shut off a switch.

The old gymnasium is also home to a ghost known for its pranks. This phantom was able to get through a set of locked doors to steal the tools of some carpenters who were working in the gym. Of course, it might have only been borrowing them: the following morning, every missing item had been returned to the exact spot where it belonged.

The Gorin Library

One room in the basement of this building is said to be haunted by the spirit of a former staff member who died accidentally on the site. Since then, the room has been known for its strange noises, smells, and unreliable lighting. People who venture into the area complain of feeling watched by unseen eyes. The library staff members generally avoid the uncomfortable room.

Blackburn Hall

Blackburn Hall is one of the newer buildings on the Millikin campus. It was constructed in 1965 to serve as a women's dormitory. Shortly after its opening, however, a ghost moved in. She is supposedly the spirit of a young student who was murdered in the late 60s. For the past 30 years, she has busied herself by interfering with anything electrical. Lights, radios, and televisions only operate as long as it pleases this phantom. When she tires of a certain program, or the sound of someone's music, she shuts off the device. Some students say that there is no use in simply turning the unit back on, for "Bonnie," as she is known, is quite stubborn. She will keep hitting the power button until the student tires of the fight.

Occasionally, Blackburn residents have encountered Bonnie's apparition in the halls. Sometimes, she will appear clearly; other times, she takes on a misty form.

Aston Hall

Aston Hall, built in 1907, is the oldest women's residence at Millikin. It is said to be occupied by the ghost of a young woman who took her own life there in the late 1940s. The white shape of this woman—visible only from the waist up—is famous for cruising through the dorm rooms, one after the other, unmindful of the walls that stand in her way. Some say that the third floor was actually closed down once, because of the spirit. Residents had been encountering her so often that they refused to stay in their rooms.

The Meridian Coffee House

The old building at number 10, East Broadway Street, in Alton, Illinois, has had many owners. There has been a dentist there, a lawyer and even a justice of the peace. For a time, it was an antique shop. More than once, it was a beauty salon. Today, the structure houses the Meridian Coffee House—and a ghost.

The current owners of the Meridian, Brenda French and Scott Baalman, bought the building in late 1997, but did not realize that they were "sharing" it until they began to renovate the following spring. Suddenly, in the building where they had felt comfortable for months, Brenda and Scott had the eerie sensation of being followed around and watched. Others who were helping with the renovations also felt nervous—particularly on the second floor—and told of hearing strange rapping sounds coming, seemingly, from within the walls. The day before the renovated coffee house was to open, Brenda even caught a glimpse of the ghost: she saw a male figure in a striped shirt sitting in one of the small, second floor rooms. The apparition lasted for only a moment before vanishing.

After the coffee house opened, the spirit continued to make its presence felt in a number of ways to staff and customers alike. The most fascinating experience took place in the summer of 1998, and was caught by the shop's security camera. The camera was aimed at the front door, with a monitor in the upstairs office. One evening just after closing time, Brenda was in the office and happened to look up at the screen. She saw her daughter, Nicole, and Scott carrying the small sidewalk tables indoors. She also saw a man in a striped shirt walk in directly behind them, and proceed to the staircase. She heard footsteps on the stairs outside the office door. She went looking for the man to tell him that the business was done for the day, but could find no one in the building. Downstairs, Scott and Nicole assured Brenda that no one had come in the door behind them. She had simply witnessed the latest appearance of their ghost.

"We decided to look at it sympathetically," Scott would later tell paranormal researcher and writer, Troy Taylor. "We knew that something was here and we didn't want to just boot it out. We told the ghost that we didn't want to get rid of it, we just asked that it try not to scare anybody or hurt anybody. As long as it was okay with that, it could stay."

And so, a spectral deal was struck at number 10, East Broadway Street, in Alton, Illinois, and the constant change in ownership has ceased.

Chapter 9

ASSORTED MYSTERIES

Ghosts can be unpredictable, and there are many stories that refuse to fit into tidy categories. Equally frustrating is the fact that while searching for tales about spirits, you will inevitably encounter a few strange-but-true accounts of other paranormal phenomena, which, while not exactly ghostly, are too good to leave out of such a book as this.

Here are the eerie extras that have been woven into the rich tapestry of supernatural legends in Illinois.

Bloody Mary Worth

No slumber party is complete without a good scare. The spooky story, the amateur seance, the Ouija board, the game of "Bloody Mary"—these things never go out of style, and Bloody Mary seems to be enjoying particular popularity at the moment. The game has been featured on television, in books and in movies, and the Internet has a plethora of sites explaining how to play the game in its different versions.

The most common version goes as follows: Enter a darkened bathroom alone. Lock the door, turn out the lights and place lighted candles to your right and left in front of the mirror. Gaze into the mirror, and chant "Bloody Mary" three times. If the ritual has been performed correctly, Mary's grotesque, blood-drenched visage will appear, and she will reach out of the mirror to scratch your eyes out and tear your face. Her appearance has never been proven, but people have been known to run out of the bathroom screaming, never to breathe a word of what they saw.

Hysterics, histrionics or supernaturally induced fear? No one but the person who summoned Mary can know.

Other variations of the ritual require that the chant be repeated 13 times, 35 times, or 100 times. In some cases, you must spin around while calling Mary; in others, it's necessary to declare belief in the hag before she'll put in an appearance. Even her moniker can change: she is known as "Bloody Mary," "Hell Mary" and, occasionally, "Mary Worth." This last name sheds some light on what may be her true beginnings—and leads the brave researcher to a 19th-century witch in Lake County, Illinois.

The story goes that Mary Worth was a notoriously evil woman who practiced her witchcraft on a farm just west of Gurnee. Her wicked behavior reached its peak during the Civil War era, when

Worth delighted in capturing runaway slaves. The slaves would remain in the barn, chained mercilessly to the rough wooden wall, until their captor saw fit to torment and kill them during one of her satanic rituals.

Stories of what went on at the Worth farm spread, until finally the people of the community could ignore them no longer. Infuriated by Worth's monstrous behavior, and perhaps fearing for their own safety, the citizens formed a vigilante mob. Worth was dragged from her home and tied to a stake where, in the true tradition of dispensing with witches, she was burned to death. The mob then proceeded to torch the barn where Worth had committed so many of her atrocities.

At this point, the story of Mary Worth splits in two. One version has it that Worth's body was buried in St. Patrick's Cemetery which, to this day, is frequently visited by those who wish to conjure or catch a glimpse of the witch's spirit. Others contend that, because it would have been highly unlikely for a known witch to have had a Christian burial, Worth cannot possibly be interred in St. Patrick's Cemetery. The second version of the story thus proposes that Mary must have been buried on her own property.

Many decades ago, a man and a woman purchased the Worth farm, which by that time contained a new home that had been constructed on the old foundation of the barn where the witch had kept her prisoners and her diabolical secrets. The couple was aware of the place's gruesome history, which by this time also included the suicide of a young girl, but was not superstitious. Interested only in making the farm productive, they set about cleaning up the land in preparation for a planting crop of oats. There wasn't much to clear from the field, but one small, square stone was quite difficult to dislodge. Once they had managed to remove it, they put the symmetrical rock at the front door of their house, to use as a step.

And that, as they say, is when all hell broke loose.

Suddenly, objects in the house began moving about on their own. Plates that were securely mounted on the wall would jump out of their stands and smash on the floor. Locks seemed to slide into place by themselves, and several times the wife found herself locked helplessly in the house or in the new barn. For years, the inexplicable, unnerving and often threatening events continued—and the couple was afraid they knew why. They felt that, by clearing the strange, square stone out of their oat field, they may have unwittingly moved the marker from Mary Worth's true grave.

The husband and wife made several desperate attempts to replace the stone, but it was impossible to remember the original location exactly. The frightening phenomena continued.

In 1986, the house burned to the ground, and the Worth property was purchased by a contractor with plans to build. That deal went bankrupt, as did the next, as did the third. Eventually, the land was subdivided and several houses were constructed—but rumor has it that the home built closest to the location of Mary Worth's barn also burned, and not just once, but twice.

Perhaps the fires can be blamed on the careless use of candles, in front of a mirror, in someone's darkened bathroom.

The Shoveling Ghost of Rock Island

In the stretch of Mississippi River that divides Davenport, Iowa, and Moline, Illinois, is a piece of land called Rock Island. In April 1916, residents of a row house there reported a most intriguing and unusual ghost.

The witnesses claimed that they looked out a window one spring evening, and saw a rather unnerving sight in the common area that served as a backyard to all tenants. It was a skeleton, gleaming white in the moonlight. It did not seem interested in frightening anyone—it was too involved in the task it was performing. The skeleton was busy digging holes.

When the hard-working ghost eventually vanished, it left behind a number of shallow holes and tidy piles of dirt. The people filled in the pits, but every so often the shoveling skeleton would return to continue his excavation.

The neighbors were certain that their unsettling guest was looking for something of value, and eventually they dug up the yard themselves in search of buried treasure. Nothing of value was found, and the residents gave up.

The ghost, on the other hand, is reported still to be digging.

One Ghost or Two?

In early 20th-century Lewistown, a middle-aged farmer named John Croke Hellyer stood trial for the murder of Cora Peters, a neighbor with whom he had been friends. The two had been drinking in town one evening, and started out on the 12-mile trek toward their farms, just before midnight. They took a route often used by local people, along the railroad tracks that led out of Lewistown. It was the last time Cora Peters was seen alive. Following a search, her battered body was discovered under a trestle on the south bank of the Spoon River.

A witness came forward to testify that he had heard a couple quarreling by the tracks on the night that Cora died, and that the man had threatened to kill the woman. Based upon this testimony, and the fact that John Croke Hellyer and Cora Peters had been together that night, Hellyer was brought to trial.

In his defense, John Croke Hellyer claimed that he and Cora had been crossing the bridge when a train approached, and that they were unable to get off the tracks in time. He said that the train hit them both, knocking them off the bridge and killing Cora. The engineer of the train said that Hellyer's story wasn't true. He had been watching his route carefully that night, and would have known had the train run anyone down.

Hellyer was found guilty, and sentenced to 25 years in prison. The mostly circumstantial evidence did not hold up for long, however, and the verdict was soon overturned. And once it became apparent that the true events of that night would never be known, there emerged a ghost story as confusing and inconclusive as the case upon which it was based.

Shortly following the trial, the engineer who had denied striking Hellyer and Patterson off the bridge began making strange reports. He claimed that on several different nights, he saw a man and a woman walking down the tracks in front of his train. He blew the whistle in vain; they simply ignored the warning. The engineer desperately applied the brakes, but as the sound of screaming metal filled his ears and the train was about to mow down the oblivious pedestrians, they simply vanished.

The engineer's story spread and soon other people were coming forward to corroborate it. It wasn't long before pedestrians were using other routes to and from Lewistown, in order not to risk meeting the increasingly famous spectral couple.

For a time, the talk died down. When the story resurfaced in the 1960s, it had changed to include only the ghost of Cora Peters. One engineer claimed that she had appeared before him on the tracks every night, until one time he could not stop the train from colliding with her transparent figure. After that, she appeared only once a year, at midnight on the anniversary of her death.

Fascinating? Yes. Creepy? Yes. And confusing? Absolutely. Upon hearing the story, one has to wonder why the ghosts started out as a couple when, at that point, John Croke Hellyer, though perhaps wronged, was still alive. Was the engineer who reported the sightings perhaps plagued by self-doubt regarding his testimony? Were the visions on the track simply a manifestation of his uncertainty? And did his stories then become planted in the minds of the locals, thereby inspiring further sightings? Furthermore, why did the story change to include only the spirit of Cora Peters at a time when John Croke Hellyer would likely have passed on too?

Whether it serves as an example of phantoms or folklore, there is no denying that the story of the mysterious specter on the tracks is one of Fulton County's most interesting tales.

A Promise Kept

In 1955, the Wohead family moved into a large house in Naperville, Illinois. It must have seemed perfect. The family's new home was conveniently close to downtown, it had a picturesque backyard in which the children could play, and it even came with a built-in "grandmother": the kindly 88-year-old landlady lived on the main floor. The elderly woman no doubt loved having children in her home again, and frequently climbed the stairs to visit the Woheads, often bringing a special homemade dessert with her.

Michael Wohead had only one concern. His children loved to play in the ancient, vine-covered grape arbor behind the house. Wohead worried that it might be unsafe, and went out one afternoon to inspect the structure. He tried with all his strength to shake it, but found the latticework to be much more solid than it appeared. Wohead's fears that the children would bring it crashing down around them disappeared.

Later that day, the elderly landlady approached Wohead. She had seen him testing the arbor and wanted to put his mind at ease. "Don't worry about that grape arbor," she said. "I'll take it down. Your children won't be hurt by it." Wohead assured the woman that the arbor seemed stable, and that he was no longer concerned. Still, she insisted that the safety of the children was paramount, and that she would see to it the structure was removed from their play area.

Sadly, Michael Wohead would have no more conversations with his landlady. She passed away within days, and as the Wohead family prepared to attend her funeral, the matter of the grape arbor was likely the last thing on their minds.

Suddenly, as the first note of the angelus bell rang out from the landlady's nearby church, the family heard a tremendous crash.

The sound came from the backyard, and they all rushed to the window to see what had happened.

The grape arbor was destroyed. On a perfectly calm day, at a time when all the children were safely indoors, the structure that Michael Wohead had been unable to budge with all his might had simply collapsed upon itself.

In the months that followed, the Woheads often felt their landlady's grandmotherly presence in their home. Many times, they heard her footsteps on the stairs. But what they would remember best about the elderly woman was that she had shown concern for the children and seen fit to keep a promise—all the way from the other side of the grave.

The Snowball-Throwing Spook

The *St. Louis Globe-Democrat* ran an article in the 1880s, in which a pioneer of Hancock County related a strange story that had taken place some 40 years earlier.

In the winter of 1844–45, a boy named Alexander Kirk went to spend the night with some school friends, whose last name was Groves. Before the boys went to bed, Mr. Groves asked them if they would make a trip out to the barn to check on the stock. The young fellows did as they were told. Nothing was amiss in the barn, but as Alex and the other lads began to walk back across the farmyard to the house, they received quite a shock.

A hard-packed snowball suddenly struck Alex squarely between the shoulders. The boys spun around to face the culprit—the coward had given no warning—but the night was dark and no one could be seen. A shower of snowballs came flying out of the blackness, and the boys turned and ran for the house. The white bullets kept coming, thrown with brute force and deadly precision, and each one was aimed directly at young Alex. Finally, the boys reached safety. They threw open the farmhouse door and spilled into the kitchen, all speaking at once about the unseen assailant.

The boys finally calmed down enough to make themselves understood. Concerned, and determined to discover the hidden rascal on his property, Mr. Groves gathered the men of the household and went to search the yard. They had been looking for several minutes and found nothing, when Alex Kirk stepped outside to check on their progress. As soon as the boy had shut the door behind him, snowballs began to strike him again in rapid succession. Seeing the stream of white missiles, the men ran to his aid. Even in the confusion, they could not help but realize that Alex was the sole target of the attacker: none of the rest of them were hit by the snowballs. One of the Groves boys tried to protect his friend by using his own body to shield Alex's back. Somehow, the snowballs still managed their furious assault on the bruised lad's shoulders. The Groves boy received only one rather glancing blow.

The night was pitch black, but the group was eventually able to see that the snowballs were coming from an area in the trees about 100 yards from the barn. A slight, eerie glow emanated from the spot, and the men set off in pursuit of the enemy. When they came close to the trees, however, they stopped in stunned silence. A tall, white figure glided out from the shadowy cover. The creature was surrounded by a sulfurous light, and warned them back with a single gesture of its long, bony hand. The threatening motion was followed by another violent shower of snowballs, thrown with greater force than any human was capable of. The men and boys had seen enough, and retreated quickly to the house.

The Groves's home was pelted with the icy projectiles all night. At sunrise, the assault ended. A few members of the family cautiously ventured outside to survey the damage, and found the yard filled with hundreds of the solid, round balls.

Mrs. Amanda Cain was the pioneer who told the story to the paper. She said that young Alex Kirk definitely suffered ill effects because of the attack. "Alex was very sore about the back and shoulders for weeks after the occurrence and, in fact, never was himself again. Although strong and full of life at the time, he was soon afterward lowered into the grave."

Mrs. Cain would have known: Alex was her mother's brother. He would have grown up to be her uncle, had he not been cruelly singled out for target practice by a bizarre, frightening, snowball-throwing ghost.

Louis Boston Returns

In January 1890, one Hancock County newspaper reported on a most sensational event that had taken place near Carthage. The headlines fairly jumped off the page:

An Alleged Apparition Near Carthage, ILL, greatly excites timid Residents!

It is Said to be the Spirit of a Good Young Man, Recently Deceased!

Exciting Adventures with the Harmless Spook—A Shadow from the Grave!

The recently deceased "good young man" was Louis C. Boston, a person of upstanding character who had passed away the previous Thanksgiving. On his deathbed, Louis had made a heartfelt profession of faith, and wished that a number of other young fellows in the area would begin following more righteous paths. Having expressed his wish, Louis expired—but it was not long before he was seen again.

A few weeks later, a man named August Wright was in his barn feeding the horses, when he was startled by the apparition of a man dressed in long, white robes. When Wright called out to the figure, it faded from sight. Four nights later, as Wright drove home from church through the deserted countryside, he met the figure once more. This time, it stepped into the middle of the road, blocking Wright's path and terrifying his horses. The animals reared and whinnied, but the specter confidently caught each one by the bridle, and soothed them with soft words. "Whoa, Charlie, whoa, Frank," it said. The animals recognized their names and settled into a wary silence. The ghost then climbed up into the buggy and turned its attention to August Wright.

"Why Aug!" the spirit declared. "Don't you know Louis Boston? Shake hands with me." Wright was shaking with fear, but took the proffered hand. Later, he would describe it as feeling as cold and clammy as that of a corpse. If Wright recoiled, the phantom seemed not to notice his reaction. It continued to speak.

"I want to talk to you," said Boston's ghost, "and if you will only listen to me a moment I will never bother you again." Wright then listened as the wraith recited messages, mostly of a religious nature, to be delivered to a number of people. Eventually, Louis Boston announced to Wright that "the angels were calling him," and he said good-bye to his old friend.

Although August Wright told several people of his encounters with the ghost of Louis Boston, he strangely refused to pass on the messages which had been entrusted to him. Rueben Boston, Louis's father, later commented to a reporter, "Louis... was a good boy and he had the welfare of his young friends at heart. I wish Aug Wright would tell you what Louis told him so you can print it. I believe he has wonderful things to tell."

That may have been, but no one was ever to know for sure. Aug Wright remained silent, and Louis Boston apparently never found a third party willing to deliver his messages from the other side.

The Running Woman

One Saturday afternoon in Decatur during the Depression, a boy and his friends were given a lucrative task. The boy's uncle had a large backyard, which contained, among other things, an old cistern that had been filled over the years with all manner of household debris. If the kids cleaned the old tank out a bit, the uncle offered, they could keep whatever treasures they found— including pop bottles, which would fetch two cents apiece. It was a great deal for the boys, who were eager to earn a little extra money. They found a spade and got to work.

Within a few hours they had already collected several bottles, which they piled carefully to the side. Then the boy whose turn it was to dig pried up something that sent him scrambling out of the hole. It was a skull—a human skull. The group stared down in amazement at their find, and pondered what to do next.

They eventually decided to dig a little further in the same spot. Within a short time, the kids had unearthed a rib cage, a spine, and several long bones. The boy decided that it was time to tell his uncle.

The man came out of the house to investigate, and was clearly shocked at what the kids had excavated. As it happened, he was a bootlegger, and was thus quite anxious to keep the police off his property, so he instructed his nephew and the others to put the remains back where they found them and not to breathe a word about them. The boy's uncle paid the group extremely well for the afternoon's work and gave the friends a word of advice: "Forget about it."

The boy might have for awhile, but he soon saw something that set him wondering about the identity of the person who lay in that undignified grave.

In the evening some weeks later, the young fellow was walking down the street that led to his uncle's home. In that neighborhood, there was one very unusual little house. It was unusual, because it always appeared smartly painted and well maintained although it had been vacant for a number of years. It looked as if someone lived there, when no one did. Sometimes the boy and his friends would walk up to the place and peer in the windows. The interior had a similar, well-kept appearance: its walls were neatly papered and its floors always seemed freshly swept. Still, although the house looked inviting, it felt evil. Perhaps it was a trap, waiting to catch someone with its friendly disguise.

On this particular evening, the boy saw a woman come tearing out the door of the house and run down the side porch that led to the street. Her heels pounded on the wooden floor as she ran. The boy stood carefully out of her way, for she was traveling at such a speed that she nearly fell as she came flying off the bottom step and turned to head up the sidewalk. The woman hurried on her way, her skirt flapping wildly around her legs. When she was about a quarter block ahead of the boy—he wondered if she was running to catch a bus—the woman disappeared. The young fellow couldn't help but notice that she vanished while passing his uncle's property, at a spot directly opposite the old cistern.

About four months later, the boy was walking along the same street at dusk. This time, he was with his grandfather. Again the woman came out of the house in a desperate run. Again her heels clattered loudly on the wooden porch. Again she nearly fell as she turned the corner, and again she vanished as she passed the old cistern. What made this experience unique for the young fellow was that his grandfather had seen it all, too. If there had been any doubt about the reality of the ghost in the boy's mind, it vanished as quickly as the ghost itself, for now another person had seen it.

The lad would see the rushing wraith one more time, but not until a number of years had passed. In 1948, when he revisited his old neighborhood, he was a grown man. He found himself lamenting the many changes that had been made to the homes and yards. Despite the altered face of the neighborhood, the man knew where the tidy little house used to be, and as he came close to the lot, the somewhat faded shadow of a woman turned onto the street ahead of him, hitting the sidewalk in a dead run. He watched her dash up the block, knowing that she would go only so far. That night, when she disappeared, she disappeared forever. The man never saw her again.

Whether the woman was running from something or to something will never be known. The neighborhood has been redeveloped, and it is too late to discover the identity, or even the gender, of the body that lay in the cistern. Whether there was some sort of connection between the skeleton in the cistern and the ghost of the running woman is something that was never discovered, but always suspected, by the young man of Decatur.

Galena's Ghostly History

In his book, *Ghosts of Galena*, which was published in 1995, author Daryl Watson wrote, "Ghosts! Are there really ghosts? Do they really haunt houses? And are any of those haunted homes in Galena?"

The answer, as it turns out, is a resounding "yes!" Every community has its invisible population of departed souls, and historic Galena is no exception. In fact, judging by Watson's convincing collection of stories, Galena may even be a city more haunted than most.

Daryl Watson is the executive director of the Galena/Jo Daviess County Historical Society and Museum. His book grew out of an interest in both history and mystery. Digging through the archives for old news accounts of ghost stories seemed the logical thing to do, when Watson and his staff began to suspect that the very museum they worked in was haunted.

The mischief began in 1989, when the staff members began hearing strange footsteps in the historic 1858 mansion. The noises could never be explained, and the curious men and women who heard them decided to start a specific computer file to keep track of the episodes. It began "almost as a joke," according to Watson, but would eventually provide him with a comprehensive account of the odd phenomena. Over the next two years, the staff members recorded bumping and shuffling noises, an inexplicably swaying chandelier, seemingly endless footsteps, an invisible force playing the piano, mysterious rapping, and the loud sounds of furniture being moved about.

Galena, Illinois. A statue of Ulysses S. Grant overlooks his former home.

One of the most compelling episodes of supernatural activity took place in January 1991, when the museum was hosting a VIP reception. Watson described the scene:

It started when one of the waitresses serving champagne to the arriving guests suddenly and inexplicably dropped her entire tray, sending the bubbly liquid all over the floor. Little attention was paid, however, and the mess was quickly cleaned up. But it wasn't more than 10 minutes later when a second server suddenly noticed the full glasses on her tray begin to tremble. Before she could steady things, the glasses and tray tumbled to the floor.

The unfortunate servers were scolded for their carelessness, but it soon became apparent that they were not at fault. Daryl Watson was standing in the museum's gift shop when his attention was caught by a tray holding a number of champagne glasses that was sitting alone on a counter. Though nothing visible was disturbing the glasses, they began to shake. More than half had fallen to the floor before anyone could stop them.

The ghost was not finished. As Watson stood in a reception line awaiting the last group of guests, the glasses began to shake on the tray of the server standing next to him. The young woman quickly grasped the tray with both hands and held it tightly. Despite her concentrated efforts, however, the champagne ended up on the floor. "We were all incredulous," Watson later wrote.

Because they worked for a museum and historical society, Daryl Watson and his staff had long recognized the value of ghost stories as part of the folklore and culture of an area. But now there was an immediate reason to take an interest in the supernatural activity in Galena. The research eventually led to Watson's entertaining and intriguing book. It is composed of newspaper stories dating back to 1845 as well as contemporary, first-hand accounts.

The historical tales are fascinating on several levels. They provide a look, not only at the ghosts, but also at the language and attitudes of different times. One fine example is the excerpt from the August 13, 1875 edition of the *Galena Daily Gazette:*

A female apparition has been cutting up capers of late, in the vicinity of Marshal O'Leary's house. The other evening that official repaired to the barn for the purpose of taking care of his horse, and while in the act of entering the stable door, he plainly saw by the light of the moon, the figure of a woman, dressed in a suit of ghostly white, and gazing full at him from out a pair of flaming eyes. Just at that instant the Marshal bethought himself of urgent business that required his immediate attention, and dropping his pail of water, he quickly made tracks for the house. Placing himself in front of a window, he watched for future developments, and in the course of time distinctly saw the apparition emerge from the barn and walk across the lot toward the wood-house. In view of the fact that it was only a woman (who couldn't vote, dead or alive) the Marshal mustered up courage, and buckling on his insignia of office, he stepped out of the door and cautiously approached the wan figure, which immediately vanished into thin air and was seen no more that night.

Ghost stories remained a popular news item in Galena throughout the years. They were so popular, that the December 28, 1888 edition of the *Galena Gazette* felt obliged to admonish its readers in the following way: "The nineteenth century is drawing to a close, and it is about time that superstition and the fears arising from it were giving place to a little common sense and reason." That said, the article went on to recount reluctantly the legend of haunted mines in the vicinity. The story concluded with the statement, "We simply state the facts, and request that the reader accept them for what they are worth."

People loved the ghost stories, so despite the newspaper's appeal for "common sense and reason," it continued to report on the paranormal events of the community. And the appeal of a ghost story was doubtless increased when a public figure was involved. In 1909, the *Daily Gazette* had some fun at the expense of an unnamed, but obviously prominent, citizen in an article headlined "No Graveyard Ghosts For Him." The article described a "well-known Galena business man, ex-alderman, member of a prominent lodge, baseball fan, [and] enthusiastic hunter," who "preferred to add two more long weary miles to his journey" one night, rather than to take a shortcut through a cemetery after dark. The man may have been wise to do so, for by this time Galena had proven itself to be quite a haunted little burg.

One particularly intriguing tale from 1907 involved a specter that repeatedly traveled a route from Horseshoe Mound to Shot Tower Hill. The apparition, which carried a lantern to light its way, was believed to be a railroad man who was killed when two trains collided on the Illinois Central tracks. Demonstrating that the city's spirits are enduring as well as plentiful, this particular ghost seems to have been active in recent years. Daryl Watson related the story of one motorist:

Well, one day Bruce and his friend were coming around [Horseshoe] Mound on their way home. They had done it a hundred times before and nothing unusual had ever happened. But this time was incredibly different. As they rounded that curve, Bruce saw a human face and body materialize and hover outside the windshield of his car! It was not a distinct face—someone that they could identify—but it was definitely a human face. It had not only a head, but legs and arms; and it appeared to be sort of a smoky-gray color. It hovered in front of the windshield and then flew up over the car, disappearing as mysteriously as it had appeared!

The haunted home of the Galena Historical Society and Museum, where Daryl Watson's book, Ghosts of Galena, *began.*

The story of the ghost of Horseshoe Mound is the first of many contemporary tales in Watson's collection. These accounts are generally set in historic buildings and homes in Galena, including one small cottage that dates back more than 150 years. Not long after one couple purchased the home, the woman was awakened one night by the sound of footsteps. She opened her eyes to a most amazing sight.

Catherine suddenly awoke... [and] looked over to see in the dim light what appeared to be the figure of a young adolescent Indian. This was not your typical North American Indian, but rather one with features more Central or South American. He had long black hair, bronze skin, and was of a very petite and fine-boned stature. His lightweight, simple garment was light-colored, and he appeared to be wearing a small head-covering, but Catherine wasn't sure.

The spirit was never seen again, although his presence was sensed. The mystery of why a Central or South American Indian would be haunting a cottage in Galena remains unsolved.

People residing in other historic Galena homes have reported a myriad of paranormal experiences to Daryl Watson. One man found that no matter how often or how carefully he turned off the lights in his home, one or two would always come back on. Another woman watched in amazement on several occasions as a cookbook flew off her kitchen shelf and fell to the floor. In the same home, disembodied voices were often heard coming from one of the bedrooms.

One family who lived in an early 19th-century home dealt with a spirit that liked to tilt carefully hung pictures. The ghost even turned one favorite photo upside-down. There was other strange activity, too. Once, the mantle clock stopped on the exact date and time of death of a previous owner of the house.

The resident specter of one old brick house liked to play bagpipes late into the night. In another historic home, family members who had opened a bed and breakfast found that they were hosting a few uninvited guests. They would occasionally hear voices that couldn't be explained, and one spring they experienced something particularly shocking. The episode was described in *Ghosts of Galena:*

Bonnie and her husband had reopened the original basement stairway immediately below the main stairway leading to the second floor. This had been sealed off and enclosed many years previously and the space used as a closet.

It was late, her husband was already upstairs sleeping and Bonnie was going around turning off lights and locking up for the night. The only lights on were little electric candle lights in the window that were left on all the time. As Bonnie walked past the "new" basement stairway she suddenly froze. There was a woman walking up from the basement! It was a woman who appeared to be 40 - 50 years of age. Bonnie could clearly make her out from the window lights still on. The sight was all the more startling because the woman was dressed in 19th-century period clothing. She wore a brown and white gingham check dress. Her hair—in fact everything about her—was definitely 19th century. At this point Bonnie caught herself, blinked, and looked twice, but the woman was gone! She had disappeared into thin air!

Watson also told the story of one other Galena guest house, where lodgers who stayed in a certain bedroom would often awaken to find the apparition of a benevolent nun hovering over them.

As for the ghost in the museum, Watson reports that all has remained quite quiet since 1991. Perhaps the spirit is at rest now, having accomplished its mission. After all, if one can believe in ghosts, it's not that much of a leap to consider that this one might have simply wanted to pique Daryl Watson's interest—and convince him to write his book, documenting the history of the ghosts of Galena.

The Headless Horseman of Illinois

Forget *The Legend of Sleepy Hollow*. In southern Illinois, near McLeansboro, the people speak of the legend of Lakey's Creek. It is a tale certainly as enduring, if not as well known, as Washington Irving's famous thriller.

More than 150 years ago, a quiet and simple man named Lakey settled on a piece of land near the creek which now bears his name. Lakey was building a little cabin for himself, and everyday the neighbors who passed by saw him working diligently on his project. One evening, a few people noticed that the man was nearly finished—he was busy shingling the roof with some large clapboards he had cut from a nearby oak tree.

But the cabin was never completed. The next morning, Lakey's neighbors found him dead. The man's lifeless body was propped up against the stump of the oak tree. His head was some distance away, in a decaying pile of leaves. Lakey's own ax, caked with gore, had apparently been the murder weapon. It was lodged deeply in the tree stump against which part of the man lay.

Lakey had no family that anyone knew of, so the people of the community simply buried the man beside his cabin.

The hard-working pioneer who had never been idle in life soon showed that he was not one to rest in the grave, either. The very day after his simple funeral service, his gruesome specter began to appear.

Two men who were traveling on horseback were approaching Lakey's Creek from the east, when suddenly a terrifying apparition overtook them. It was a headless horseman, riding a coal black steed. As the frightened men coaxed their horses to go faster, the horrible phantom kept pace. As they entered the shallow part of the stream, so did the ghost. Midway across, however, the specter turned downstream, and faded into the mist.

The two frightened men agreed to never speak of their experience, lest it be thought that they had lost their minds. Their concern was needless, however, for within days, two other men had experienced the same headless terror. It soon became common knowledge that Lakey's ghost was haunting Lakey's Creek.

In the decades that followed, many would encounter the headless corpse and his midnight animal. When a bridge was finally built across the creek, the phantom, keeping up with the times, used it. Still, he would turn downstream in the middle of the concrete structure, and disappear as he sped into the distance.

Lakey's killers were never found, and no one ever understood what motive anyone might have had for attacking this man who had no money and no enemies. Whether the pioneer's ghost was trying to find the murderers, or to explain to passers-by what happened on that night, will likely never be known. The spirit's appearances have become rather infrequent in recent years. Still, the story of the headless horseman of Illinois will be told for many years to come.

The Hancock Hanging

In the 1880s, an article in the *St. Louis Globe-Democrat* recalled the events of the "one legal hanging" that took place in Hancock County, Illinois. The paper stated that "in 1839 Fielding Frame was launched into eternity at Carthage by due process of the law." The charge against Frame had been murder, and he had been found guilty despite the best efforts of his three lawyers, one of whom was Abraham Lincoln. The date of execution had been set for Saturday, May 18, 1839.

A crude gallows was constructed in an open field near Carthage. The location had been chosen specifically because of the surrounding hills, which formed a sort of natural amphitheater. The authorities were apparently expecting a crowd, and the people of the county did not disappoint them. They came from miles around on the appointed day, and crowded the grassy hills. Everyone was eager to witness the horrid, but historic, event.

The scaffold was nothing more than two upright posts with a crossbar. A rope dangled from it, ominously waiting for Frame to make his appearance. When at noon the prisoner was brought in from the old stone jail, the grim task was performed unceremoniously. A local minister mumbled a few words. Fielding Frame was then placed in the bed of a wagon, with the noose around his neck and a black cap over his head. At the sheriff's signal, the whip was snapped upon the team of horses. The animals sprang forward, and jerked the wagon out from under the gallows. Frame fell.

It was then that the witnesses began to wish they had never come. The *Globe-Democrat* reported that the poor wretch slowly strangled to death, and that in his frightful struggles the black cap became deranged, exposing the contortions of the features. A peculiar gurgling sound issued from the victim's throat. Many ladies fainted and the most hardened men turned pale.

The bungling of the affair did not stop at Frame's botched execution. Showing what the *Globe-Democrat* described as "amazing disregard for decency and security," the officials immediately buried the body on the very location where the man had been hanged. The grave was not particularly deep, either, which made easy work for the grave robbers who, that very night, performed the final indignity on Frame's corpse. Given the circumstances, it should have been expected that the man's spirit would not rest.

One evening not long after the execution, two farmers were walking the long route into Carthage. In order to save a little time, they cut through the pasture in which the gallows stood. Disquieted by the morbid reminder of the execution, the men picked up their pace a bit. They spoke in hushed voices about the grisly sight they had seen there. As if cued by their discussion, a horrid and all too familiar sound assailed their ears.

It was a choking, gurgling sound, as if some human being was strangling. The sounds came from the gallows, and with trembling steps the two now thoroughly frightened men crept that way. With a shriek one of them cried out: "My God! It's Frame— it's Frame! He's being hung again—only it's just his head!"

There, dangling from the rope, was a human head. Its black cap had fallen to the ground, and the face resembled that of Fielding Frame, although it was "so disfigured with agony as to be almost unrecognizable." The swollen tongue protruded grotesquely, and the eyes bulged from their sockets. All the while the head hung there, it produced hideously liquid gasping sounds. The farmers were limp with terror, when finally the vision ended. The dreadful face simply turned into a white mist and floated away, dragging the rope behind it.

It was said that some others who passed through the field at later dates reported hearing the same tortured choking sounds, but no one was ever again witness to the ghastly apparition of Fielding Frame's head.

Frank Leavy's Haunted Handprint

On the morning of Good Friday, April 18, 1924, the firefighters of Chicago's Engine Company 107 and Truck Company 12 were busying themselves with a bit of spring cleaning. For the moment, there was nothing else to do, but the men were on full alert because of a four-alarm blaze at the Union Stockyards. The stockyard was outside their territory, but it affected them nonetheless: so many of the city's fire-fighting companies had been called there, that the men of Company 107 had little hope of backup should another fire break out.

One of the men on duty was Francis X. Leavy. He was known as Frank to all his friends. The usually cheerful fellow appeared lost in melancholy that day, as he washed the glass panes of the fire-house door with soapy water. Edward McKevitt, a fellow firefighter, asked why Leavy was blue. Leavy sighed deeply and rested his wet hand against the window. "This is my last day with the fire department," he stated dully.

McKevitt was taken aback. He knew that Leavy had made no plans to quit his job, and did not understand the meaning of the morose statement. Before he could ask for an explanation, however, the alarm bell rang. The men were being called to a burning office building named Curran Hall, which was about two miles away.

They arrived to discover a virtual inferno. The structure was engulfed in flames. Some of the men of Truck Company 12 were ordered to the roof, where they were to chop holes that would allow the thick smoke to escape. Frank Leavy was in another group of men sent to the second floor, where the heart of the fire was suspected to be. Each of the brave firefighters followed the orders without question.

After several minutes, the supervisors on the scene noticed with horror that the outside wall of the building was about to collapse. "Get out! Get out!" they screamed, as bricks began to hit the ground. The men tried to race down the fire escapes, but the warning had come too late. With a deafening sound, the wall crumbled, taking the firefighters down with it. Eight men lost their lives in the crash. Hours later, the remaining firefighters pulled the bodies of their colleagues from the massive pile of debris, and noted that only Frank Leavy's face was still recognizable.

The next day, Edward McKevitt was at the station house relating his version of the terrible event. As he was telling the other firefighters about Frank Leavy's startling premonitory remark, McKevitt happened to look at the glass that Leavy had been cleaning. There, on the pane where Leavy had rested his hand, was a well-defined print.

McKevitt rose to take a closer look at the image, and wiped at it with a sponge. The handprint did not budge. Someone else tried scrubbing at the glass with ammonia, but found it had no effect. One of the men even attempted to scrape the impression off with a razor blade, but to no avail. Frank Leavy had left his mark upon the firehouse, and it appeared to be very permanent.

The story spread through the city, and numerous people showed up to have a look at the remarkably clear print of the dead man's hand. Someone from City Hall brought a copy of Leavy's thumbprint when he visited, and declared that the match was exact. An expert from the Pittsburgh Plate Glass Company— the manufacturer of the window—produced a special chemical compound that would remove anything from a window. The expert eventually gave up and left, and Frank Leavy's stubborn handprint remained.

Eventually, the fervor died down. The blemished pane of glass was left in place out of respect for the dead, and out of a belief that it was unwise to interfere with something that, truly, no one understood.

For two decades, new firefighters who were assigned to that station were always shown the glass and told the mysterious tale of Frank Leavy's death. Then, on April 18, 1944—exactly 20 years after the strange event—a delivery boy accidentally threw a rolled-up newspaper through the pane of glass, and shattered it.

Perhaps the date of the accident was a coincidence. Perhaps Frank Leavy felt that 20 years was long enough for the unusual monument to last. Or perhaps he was simply stepping aside for another.

The very next year, Leavy's son, Frank, Jr., joined the fire department. There is little doubt that the young man hoped to make his own mark there—in a less tragic and supernatural way.

The Silver Bullet Process

In the mid-19th century, near Plymouth, Illinois, a man named Abie Spivey lived a mean and bitter existence. Spivey was a sullen man who kept to himself and rarely spoke to his neighbors. The only subject that could rouse him into excited conversation was the occult.

Abie Spivey believed in witches. He considered himself a terrific expert on them. He would go on at length about the evil hags and the secret methods by which they could be fought. Abie knew: he claimed that he had been successfully warding off a veritable onslaught of witches, which he believed to be plaguing Hancock County, for a long time. Abie Spivey's neighbors listened to his rants, not out of politeness, but out of fear. The people of the community knew that anyone as unbalanced as Spivey could arbitrarily decide to single out any one of them as an enemy.

In the summer of 1843, Abie Spivey did decide that it was time to find one person upon whom to focus his hatred. His lucky charms had lost their effectiveness, and Spivey knew that it must be because of one supremely powerful witch. Spivey's cows were giving salt milk; his corn crop was growing with its roots up; his favorite coon dog died; and his oxen strayed off his property. It was clear that the witch had to be found and immediately dealt with. Abie cast a jaundiced eye around his small community and decided that the hag-in-hiding was his own sister-in-law, Mrs. Able Friend.

Abie Spivey had a secret weapon in his arsenal. Known as "the silver bullet process," it was reserved for desperate cases such as

Abie's, in which it was clear that the witch had to be killed. The victim was to draw the image of the woman in question upon a board or a tree, then fire a single silver bullet into the effigy's head or heart. It was said to be as effective as if one had fired a lead slug into the living person.

What Spivey did not know, as he worked on his crude likeness of Mrs. Friend, was that the woman was actually very ill with typhoid fever. As the smug and insane man gleefully cast a silver coin in his bullet mold, the poor woman died. Only minutes after Abie Spivey fired his silver bullet into the head of the image tacked up on the smokehouse door, a neighbor drove up to deliver the sad news.

Abie was delighted to hear of his sister-in-law's passing, and bragged to the stunned neighbor that he was responsible for her death. When the man asked how that could be, Spivey led him to the smokehouse and proudly pointed to the bullet hole in the head of his rough drawing. He explained the silver bullet process and assured the shocked fellow that he, Abie Spivey, had just rid the community of a powerful witch.

Within an hour, the neighborhood was in a state of chaos. The good people who had for so long put up with Abie Spivey's crazy notions now wanted him dealt with—immediately. When it became clear that a lynch mob was about to form, a warrant was issued for Spivey's arrest.

The authorities then executed a clever plan to prevent the unnecessary killing of the crazy old man.

Spivey, who was no doubt appalled at his neighbors' ingratitude, was taken first into custody and then into court to answer to the charge of murder. The speedy trial was held in the presence of a nearly riotous crowd, which kept demanding that the judge allow it to deal with Spivey in its own, swift fashion. The judge would have none of it though, and seemed bent upon following the letter of the law.

It took the jury of six men only 10 minutes to decide that Abie Spivey was guilty of Mrs. Friend's murder. It took the judge only a moment longer to sentence the bewildered man to be hanged by the neck until he was dead. The bloodthirsty crowd, finally appearing satisfied, dispersed.

When it seemed that the volatile situation had been defused, the pretense was dropped. The judge sternly rebuked Spivey for his foolish and dangerous superstition, and then turned him loose. Spivey, no doubt wiser from the suitable fright and grave warning, laid low for a little while before quietly returning to his farm.

Abie Spivey lived there until his death, some 20 years later. It can probably be assumed that he kept more to himself than ever, and, despite his enduring belief in witches, never risked using the silver bullet process again.

In the Nick of Time

One cold winter day, a woman from Arlington Heights was steering her car out of a parking lot into the busy traffic of a three-lane street. The pavement was covered by a sheet of ice, a fact she realized only when her vehicle began sliding completely out of her control. The woman sat helpless behind the wheel as her car skidded into the street. With sickening horror, she looked left. A red car was hurtling toward her at no less than 50 miles per hour. It could not possibly avoid hitting her.

"So I closed my eyes," she later wrote, "put my head down, and waited for the crash."

Strangely, nothing happened. When several seconds had passed, the woman opened her eyes and saw the impossible:

the red car, which had had no way of maneuvering around her vehicle, was now some distance down the street, stopped at an intersection. It had been bearing down on her from her left, but was now far off to her right. It was as though the red car had passed right through her. The woman was stunned, but regained control of her sliding car, and steered safely out of the way of traffic.

Later, still shaken and bewildered by the incident, the woman wrote to Dr. Bruce Goldberg, a psychologist, author and columnist at *FATE* magazine. "This event may not sound strange to you," she wrote, "but believe me, it was not physically possible for this to have happened. Can you explain this?"

Dr. Goldberg offered three intriguing explanations. He suggested that the woman may have experienced the teleportation of her car. He said there may have been intervention by a spiritual being. Finally, he suggested that a time traveler from the future may have interceded on the woman's behalf. "These chrononauts often function as spirit guides while in the fifth dimension," Goldberg wrote in his response.

Certainly, some force looked after the woman that day. Whether it was an angel, a spirit, or a chrononaut matters not so much as the fact that it saved her life.

The Seneca Cremation

On Christmas Eve in 1885, an old couple who lived on a fine farm near Seneca, Illinois, made paranormal history—by dying, in a most unusual fashion.

Patrick Rooney and his wife were celebrating the season, sitting at the kitchen table with a half-gallon brown jug of whiskey placed between them. When their hired man, John Larson, came in from his chores, he was invited to join them. Larson stayed in the kitchen only long enough for two drinks before deciding to retire upstairs to his bedroom. He wished the Rooneys a Merry Christmas and good-night, not knowing that it was the last time he would see them alive.

In the middle of the night, Larson awoke, certain that he had come down with a terrible cold. The man found it hard to breathe. He coughed a few times, trying to clear his throat, then fell asleep again. In the morning, he awoke early, feeling quite ill.

John Larson pulled on his clothes and crept through the still-dark house to the kitchen. He felt that a glass of water and a breath of fresh air would help him to feel a little better. The first order of business, however, was to light the kerosene lamp, so Larson tried to strike a match on the stove. It simply slid across the surface.

The hired man put his hand on the cold range and found that it was thickly coated with a greasy, sooty substance. Other surfaces in the kitchen seemed similarly covered. Alarmed, Larson went to wake his employers.

John Larson received a greater shock when he opened the Rooneys' bedroom door. There, in the dim morning light, he found Patrick Rooney lying dead on the floor. His wife was nowhere to be seen, and when Larson shouted for her, he received no answer. Clearly, it was time to get some help.

Larson quickly fed the horses, then saddled one and rode to the farm of Patrick Rooney's son, about a mile and a half distant. He delivered the news, and together the two men made the return journey. While they rode, the young Rooney speculated that his stepmother had perhaps killed the old man and then run off, but his fears of that possibility were soon dispelled. The men searched the house in the full light of day, and made a gruesome discovery.

In the kitchen, everything was black with greasy soot. Beside the kitchen table was a three- by four-foot hole in the floor, and beneath that, on the cold cellar floor, was what remained of Mrs. Rooney.

Of the once 200-pound woman, there was nothing left but a skull, a bit of vertebra, part of one foot, and a heap of cold ashes. Apart from the woman's body and the floorboards, however, nothing else had burned. Only one corner of the tablecloth showed any signs of being lightly scorched.

The coroner's inquest into Patrick Rooney's death was simple: he had succumbed to smoke inhalation. John Larson might have suffered the same fate, had his bedroom door not been closed. But what had killed Mrs. Rooney? Now that was a mystery. Her remains had been positively identified, and the coroner determined that there must have been a fire burning for several minutes at over 2500 degrees Fahrenheit to consume her so entirely. But no one had any idea what caused the fire, or an answer why the rest of the kitchen had not gone up in flames. The completely unsatisfying conclusion of the coroner's inquest was "accidental death."

The conclusion of the inquest did not result in the conclusion of speculation, however. Long after Patrick Rooney and what remained of his wife had been interred in the Roman Catholic cemetery, townspeople were still trying to solve the mystery. Many began to blame the Rooneys for their own deaths, focusing upon the fact that they had been drinking on the night of their misfortune.

"Tragic End of an Old Couple Whose Weakness was the Cause of Their Sad Demise," blared one New Year's Day headline from the *Ottawa Republican*. In a letter to the editor of the *Ottawa Free Trader*, a man wrote to remind readers that "Temperance lecturers have always told stories of the combustion of inebriates, and... theologians would add that the burning must go on eternally."

Today, the moralizing has ended, and the Rooney case is seen by some as a textbook example of a strange phenomenon known as spontaneous human combustion, or SHC. SHC is described as the high-speed consumption of the human body by intense heat, but with no apparent outside cause. This description seems to fit Mrs. Rooney's demise.

Victims of spontaneous human combustion are often women and often overweight. Temperance lecturers can satisfy themselves on one point: alcohol is often present. The combustion is usually very rapid and complete, and nearby items—even very flammable ones—are left unscorched. Another strange detail is that nearly all cases of SHC take place during winter months in the northern hemisphere.

Some theorists have tried to explain the phenomenon as being the result of an abnormal amount of electrostatic charge within a human body. The fact is, however, that SHC, and the strange death of Mrs. Rooney, remain a mystery to this day.

North America's colorful history is full of spine-tingling ghost tales that will have you checking under the bed, behind closet doors and in the basement. Haunting tales involve many well-known theatres, buildings and landmarks, many of which are still being used. Stories range from the return of long-dead relatives, to phantom footsteps in unused attics, to whispers of disembodied voices from behind the walls.

Collect the whole series!

Ghost Stories of Washington
By Barbara Smith
Seattle Underground • Yakima's Capitol Theatre
• Port Townsend's Manresa Castle • Gonzaga University and more
$10.95 U.S. • 1-55105-260-1 • 5.25" x 8.25" • 232 pages

Ghost Stories of the Rocky Mountains
By Barbara Smith
Banff Springs Hotel • Denver's Unsinkable Molly Brown • the Frank Slide
• Warren Air Force Base and more
$10.95 U.S. • 1-55105-165-6 • 5.25" x 8.25" • 240 pages

Ghost Stories of California
By Barbara Smith
Alcatraz • the Queen Mary • a historic Tinseltown hotel
• the Joshua Tree Inn and more
$10.95 U.S. • 1-55105-237-7 • 5.25" x 8.25" • 224 pages

Ghost Stories of Hollywood
By Barbara Smith
Griffith Park • Mann's Chinese Theater • John Wayne's haunted yacht
• major movie studios and more
$10.95 U.S. • 1-55105-241-5 • 5.25" x 8.25" • 224 pages

Available at your local bookseller or from Lone Pine Publishing:
U.S. 1-800-518-3541 • Fax 1-800-548-1169
Canada 1-800-661-9017 • Fax 1-800-424-7173

For other titles in our Ghost Stories Series please contact us.